Oswald Mosley
Portrait of a Leader

A. K. Chesterton

Portrait of a Leader

A. K. Chesterton

First Published by Action Press 1937

Copyright © 2019 Sanctuary Press Ltd

ISBN-13: 978-1-913176-17-4

Sanctuary Press Ltd
71-75 Shelton Street
Covent Garden
London
WC2H 9JQ

www.sanctuarypress.com
Email: info@sanctuarypress.com

To the
Blackshirts of Britain
in admiration of their
devoted service to the
Land they love and
the Leader they revere.

The Leader of "British Union"

"We count it a privilege to live in an age when England demands that great things shall be done, a privilege to be of the generation which learns to say what can we give instead of what we can take. For thus our generation learns there are greater things than slothful ease; greater things than safety; more terrible things than death.

For this shall be the epic generation which scales again the heights of Time and History to see once more the immortal lights - the lights of sacrifice and high endeavour summoning through ordeal the soul of humanity to the sublime and eternal. The alternatives of our age are heroism or oblivion. There are no lesser paths in the history of Great Nations. Can we, therefore, doubt which path to choose?

Let us tonight at this great meeting give the answer. Hold high the head of England; lift strong the voice of Empire. Let us to Europe and to the world proclaim that the heart of this great people is undaunted and invincible. This flag still challenges the winds of Destiny. This flame still burns. This glory shall not die. The soul of Empire is alive, and England again, dares to be great."

Extract from Sir Oswald Mosley's speech at Albert Hall, March 22, 1936.

Contents

Preface

I do not claim for this book that it is written in a spirit of cold detachment. No man who holds strong views about British politics would be able to summon up that spirit in a contemporary portrait of Oswald Mosley. The man and the movement of his creation break through any pretensions of neutrality. They are hated - or admired and followed with a loyalty beyond the hope, though not beyond the envy, of all other men and all other political movements in Britain to command. It would have been possible, of course, to simulate a detached attitude, but not with honesty. I am an admirer of Mosley, and ten times greater an admirer after the research necessary for the writing of this book. If its authenticity on that account be denied, the reader is at liberty to seek redress in portraits (they are plentiful) painted by Mosley's enemies. I do not think that he will stumble upon any truer likeness. In this world it is from our friends and not from our enemies that we are likely to receive most justice.

I have concentrated attention on Mosley, with only as much background sketched in as was necessary to explain his activities. Readers wishing for more detailed perspective should read James Drennan's masterly book "Oswald Mosley, B.U.F. and British Fascism." Similarly, in explaining the evolution of Mosley's view and his present policy I have left out all references, cross-references and statistics, so that the reader might be presented with a swift moving narrative. In order to fill in the gaps left by this method recourse should be had to Mosley's own book "The Greater Britain," which, in any event, nobody interested in Fascism should neglect to study. In conclusion, admitting the bias in my approach, I declare that I have set down nothing in these pages which I do not believe to be true.

A.K.C.

1 - Family Perspective

It may be said that in a very particular and intimate sense Oswald Ernald Mosley was born of the soil.

During many centuries his family has had roots in the countryside - an association clearly established for over eight hundred years, and offering fairly distinct traces back through Norman times to the Anglo Saxon settlements. When Oswald Mosley forms a mental picture of his native country, therefore, it is reasonable to suppose that the background tends to exclude the excrescences of the Industrial Revolution, being compact of what is left inviolate of its earth. His own youth would strengthen this supposition. Although London was chosen as his birthplace, the sights and sounds of the city were much less familiar to him than galloping horses and baying hounds and the good, clean things that grow in his own Staffordshire soil.

Here at the start is a factor both fortunate and important. It means that today there is advancing towards the leadership of the nation a man predisposed to look upon the nineteenth century triumphs of economic liberalism as placing a false and perilous emphasis upon industrialism and usury at the expense of agriculture and creating a lop-sided economy which accepted as permanent factors whose impermanence still lacks political recognition, even while the towns decay with the general decline of the countryside.

A believer in predestination might find much in the history of the family to suggest that fate had no intention of allowing Oswald Mosley to grow up in any other environment. There was a time, for instance, when it owned considerable land in Lancashire over which a large part of Manchester now stretches. Had this land not been sold before the expansion of the city took place it is likely that the Mosleys would have found their squiredom transformed into the responsibilities of urban landlordism, much to the advantage of their fortunes, though not without loss of another kind.

As the family at one time might have been swallowed up in the affairs of Manchester, so at another time might it have settled down permanently in London. During Elizabeth 's reign there was an ancestor - one, Sir Nicholas Mosley - who achieved considerable importance in London's civic life, becoming Lord Mayor and identifying himself with the high adventure of the time by the equipment, in defiance of orders, of a fleet for service against the Spaniards. Elizabeth was displeased with him at the outset, but nothing succeeded like success with the Queen, and when the ships returned in triumph she sent for him to confer on him the order of knighthood, together with the motto; Mos legem regit,[1] which - opponents doubtless say - admirably describes the temper of his twentieth century descendant!

Oswald Mosley, indeed, would scarcely have failed to come into his own had he been born a subject of Elizabeth. One can picture him striding across the landscape of that time as though an artist had designed it for him - a superb physical and mental specimen of a race rapturously discovering its own vigour amidst the thousand-fold possibilities of the new life then being unfolded for its opportunity and triumph. Had he been able to stay the course with the Queen (which is improbable) he would have blazed his way to victory in precisely those directions in which Essex stumbled to the block, and in any event, an age of adventurous idealism and practical patriotism must certainly have marked him down for high leadership.

The Mosleys did not stay in London. The call of the country was too strong, and they soon moved their domicile back to Lancashire and later to Staffordshire, where they settled down at Rolleston, to found a long line of Midland squires, enjoying

---

1   Custom, or precedent, rules the law.

a tranquillity and a more or less unbroken tenure that only the Civil War disturbed. During the war the family were strongly Royalist, in which cause they fought with valour. The defence of Tutbury Castle, which they owned, is an epic that belongs to history. It is believed that the castle was the only Cavalier stronghold that never fell. Cromwell occupied the family seat at Rolleston, from which vantage point he wrote to the defenders of Tutbury threatening to burn the place to the ground unless they surrendered. The threats seem only to have stimulated resistance. The head of the family at that period is reputed to have fallen at Naseby, while the family suffered some confiscation of lands which were only partially recovered at the Restoration. Apparently the sympathies of the Mosley squires remained constant, for it has been stated (in Mr. Compton Mackenzie's book) that Prince Charles stayed in the family house in Lancashire when he visited England incognito prior to the '45. The extent to which they were implicated in the Jacobite rising however, is not known.

The Moselys are not heard of again in any national sense until they produced in Sir Oswald Mosley, Bart., a man of intellectual distinction and considerable learning, who represented Staffordshire in Parliament, and expressed some powers of leadership both here and in the Midlands as a prominent Whig and Reform Bill figure. Sir Oswald Mosley was probably not a very inspired leader. His writings, revealing as they do many admirable qualities, cannot conceal the absence of anything suggesting a vital spark. It appears that by this time the family had lost the daring and enterprise of its Elizabethan and Cavalier spirit and lapsed into a somewhat ponderous pedestrianism, becoming - in the present Oswald Mosley's phrase - "lamentably respectable." Thus did it continue during the next few generations, showing much prowess in sport, but little intellectual zest and no spiritual swell. Nevertheless, there was one remarkable man who served as a symbol for Victorian England - a symbol which still survives. This was Sir Oswald Mosley, grandfather of the subject of this book.

Sir Oswald Mosley, grandfather of the present Baronet.

1 - Family Perspective

People all over the world are familiar with the figure which Englishmen love to invest with what they consider to be their supreme virtues; a figure sturdily built, although inclining a little to corpulence, with an open face full of bluff honesty, and common sense, generally exuding good nature, though in times of peril wearing an air of implacable determination calculated to make even the largest foreign dreadnought think twice before firing its broadsides; a figure who during the Great War stood symbolically in loco parentis for the men of the race - the patriotic figure, in short, of John Bull. This famous symbol, as it happens, was based upon the appearance and general characteristics of the grandfather of the man who is today representing the people of England in more than a symbolic sense and rapidly making good his claim to be their leader.

The Sir Oswald Mosley who became identified with the John Bull legend was in many ways a tremendous fellow. As a young man he was famed for his strength and athleticism, among other things achieving the distinction of being runner-up in the middle-weight boxing contest for the British title. Later his name was known from one end of the country to the other as a great agriculturalist, the family's age-long association with the soil finding in him its apotheosis. He was noted chiefly for his scientific experiments in stock-breeding. Countless prizes were won by his Shorthorn bulls and Shire horses; the former sweeping the board for years at all the principal shows. "John Bull" was a conspicuous figure on these occasions and became extremely popular with farmers, whose interests he so passionately shared, and whose outlook was so well expressed in his own personality, shrewdness, and humorous, forthright manner.

This was the man destined to play a leading part in shaping the early life of Oswald Mosley; in fact, during those early years his was the dominating male influence, due to a set of circumstances which must be set down in this place if some rather unhappy subsequent history is to be understood.

Sir Oswald Mosley's son, also an Oswald Mosley, married his second cousin, Miss Maude Heathcote, daughter of the then Member for Stafford, a man well known in the sporting world of his day. There were three children, Oswald, Edward, and John. Oswald Mosley was born on November 16, 1896. The marriage did not endure. When Oswald Mosley was five years old his parents separated, and thereafter his time was spent alternately with his mother in Shropshire and with his grandfather in Staffordshire. Between this grand old man and the boy there developed one of those great friendships from which both derive pleasure and profit, "John Bull" no doubt finding the company of the eager-spirited, tall, good-looking youngster a source of constant refreshment, while the youngster, in his turn, learnt all the ways of the countryside and picked up many a piece of wisdom about life from his shrewd elder. Unfortunately, Oswald Mosley's father - a man of very different stamp - did not get on well with his own father and seems to have resented the affection and understanding which existed between him and the boy. The resentment culminated in a quarrel which destroyed whatever slender chances there were of a happy association between himself and his son, and resulted in a virtual estrangement marked with extreme bitterness on his part. It is necessary that these facts should be recorded because many years later, when Oswald Mosley's convictions led him into another political camp, his father's sense of outrage fed upon the old bitterness and launched him into an attack on him more petulant, more childish, and more starkly unjust than any public attack ever made by a father upon his own son in the history of these islands. As will soon become clear, the onslaught betrayed in him a deplorable ignorance of the character of the son.

During these early years young Oswald Mosley led a life in no way different from that of other boys similarly circumstanced. He grew up out of doors and enjoyed all the simpler forms of country sport, being scarcely seen except in the company of dogs, guns, ferrets, and later, of horses. His association with horses began later owing to a singular incident which I set down because of the strong light it throws on the determination of the boy even before he reached his teens. Shortly before his birth his mother was involved in a carriage accident, and the result was one of those things one often reads about but rarely encounters - a prenatal neurosis. The child from the very first days could not bear the sight of horses, which filled him with an unreasoning terror out of keeping with his general manliness. He would tremble whenever they came near, and put as big a distance between himself and them as he could manage. The family treated the nervousness wisely, never remarking upon it and not so much as indicating that they noticed anything unusual.

Then one day, when he was about five, young Mosley came into the room, with his face very set and white, and announced that he wished to learn to ride. The statement was accepted as though it were entirely natural, and his mother (from whom I have had the story) arranged for the lessons to begin. The boy was closely observed as he approached the selected horse. His torment was extreme, but so was the resolution which he summoned to grapple with it, on this as on subsequent occasions. Pale and trembling, he stayed the course and won through to victory, conquering his own neurosis so thoroughly that when he came to enter the army it was the cavalry arm that he chose for his service. The indomitable spirit of the child was to become the indomitable spirit of the man.

Oswald Mosley's schooldays began at West Downs, where he describes himself as having been "intellectually competent." This is perhaps an understatement, since the impression he made on some of his contemporaries was that of a distinctly clever youngster, though with none of that precocity which brings so many people to the threshold of manhood with a neglected physique, and leaves them, before thirty, more or less intellectually barren except along the lines of their own specialised studies. Essays of the period show that at an early age he had developed the art of self-expression, while at ten, his reputation as a debater was firmly established among his school-fellows. There was one celebrated occasion when he swung the whole school round to his side by advancing the ingenious theory that the Roman Empire declined largely because its citizens took too many baths - an argument well calculated to appeal to small boys.

It is true, however, that Nature had to take special precautions to slow down young Mosley's mental processes after the age of about eleven, in order to enable him to cope with his remarkable physical growth. At fourteen he reached his full stature, becoming a young giant six feet two inches in height, so that a lull was clearly necessary in his development while he consolidated his strength.

On that account it is not surprising that his distinctions at Winchester, where he went before he was thirteen, were all athletic and sporting. He had shown at West Downs that he inherited his grandfather's skill as a boxer, and for his first three years of public-school life almost his entire energies were concentrated on this sport, in which he became very efficient. Refused permission by his headmaster to enter for the Public Schools Boxing Championship, he overcame his disappointment in characteristic fashion by turning to fencing, in which section no such prohibition existed. Here again he revealed his quickness of hand and eye, and the general excellence of his nerves, winning the Public Schools Fencing Championship with both foil and sabre at the early age of fifteen years and four months. Several records were eclipsed thereby. He was the youngest competitor to win either event and the first to win both on the same day. Another proud occasion was when he went to Eton with a team and scored fifteen hits without being touched. Small wonder that when many years afterwards he took up fencing again, purely as an exercise, Mosley should have become runner-up in the British Epée Championship for two years in succession (1932 and 1933), and been selected to represent Great Britain in the European Championship of 1935.

Mosley's athletic activities and his immense physical development, while they absorbed most of his energies, did not prevent him displaying sound average intelligence in form subjects. He was particularly interested in history, but put up a good show - if not a brilliant one - in every other study required of him. Mosley sums up his general prowess by saying; "While at Winchester I was not particularly stupid; I was certainly not in any way intellectually distinguished."

Intellectual growth seems to have been resumed soon after he left, which he did owing to an injury on the athletic field when only sixteen. While waiting to enter Sandhurst he continued his reading in history, turning his attention particularly to its political implications, and had so far recovered his earlier intellectual promise as to pass into Sandhurst first on the cavalry list - a distinction a little sullied by his being written down to fifth place at the instance of the examiners, who were appalled by Mosley's one single trait that may justly be called execrable - his handwriting. Its illegibility persists to this day. Soon after a distribution of memoranda from him to officers at his headquarters many doors simultaneously swing open and there is a solemn procession to the office of his secretary, George Sutton, who is reputed to be the only man alive who can make head or tail of what Mosley writes - and sometimes even Sutton's usually imperturbable features become full of trouble, as at a mystery that defies elucidation. It will be seen, therefore, that the young officer-cadet owes some gratitude to his examiners for their labour in penetrating into the maze of the papers which he submitted for their edification.

Mosley's choice of the Army as a career was natural. His family during many centuries had been proud to serve their King when the need arose. The awful menace of the Great War was being everywhere sensed. He was a young patriot saturated in the history of his land. There was no tale of daring in our island annuls which did not thrill his eager spirit, and his own achievement in manly sports could scarcely have left him in any doubt as to his ability to comport himself with honour in a profession that calls pre-eminently for the exercise of manly virtues. His was the spirit and outlook of the age. To serve one's country at the post of danger was a privilege for which every healthy young Briton would have died rather than foregone. Mercifully for Britain the time was fantastically remote from that unhappy future when British youth at Oxford was to communicate to the world the announcement that neither King nor Country was worth the offering of their precious lives.

Meanwhile, the young man destined in later years to challenge this and every other form of decadence that was to threaten the existence of a great and majestic peoples went to prepare for the more immediate, if not more urgent, task that was intuitively felt to lie in the very near future. Like hundreds of thousands of other young Englishmen, Oswald Mosley was superbly ready for whatever should be required in the way of service and of sacrifice.

2 - Mosley In The War

Oswald Mosley's life at Sandhurst was strenuous and happy. He took his studies seriously but still found time for his sporting interests. Among other activities he played polo for the College. He had friends. So far as that was possible in the Sandhurst world, he even had a following. Nothing happened during all this period to cause him a moment's regret in after-life. And yet, when he came to enter politics and to be feared by all the corrupt interests which he consistently challenged, it was to these days that his opponents harked back in search of discreditable incidents to use against him. Such is the democratic method invariably employed whenever a man is found too big to be put out of action in the cut-and-thrust of ordinary debate. The incident which his detractors discovered for their purpose must be described here, if only to prevent Mosley's future biographers being misled by a stupid distortion and lie.

A dispute arose between him and another cadet about some polo ponies, and since a question of principle was involved they proceeded to do something which the Oxford world of today will find just too dreadful - they fought it out with their fists. At that time of high spirits and vitality "wars" were frequent between rival factions at Sandhurst, and after the individual combat finished, with the knock-out of Mosley's opponent, the respective adherents of the two took up the matter and a grand "rag" occurred in the evening, during which young Mosley decided to seek reinforcement by climbing from one building to another, an operation he had often managed before without difficulty. On this occasion, however, he fell heavily and incurred injuries from which he soon recovered, well in time to be certified fit for active service, and to be passed out of Sandhurst with the first batch of his category at the beginning of the war.

Absurd as it may seem, Mosley's political opponents years afterwards made use of this entirely creditable, if trifling, incident in order to try and damage his election chances. They said he had been "thrown out" of a window and dared even to allege that his war injuries, honourably incurred in the service of his country, had no origin apart from his Sandhurst fall. When the average politician is in fear, there is no absurd lie he will refuse to tell in order to advance his career, no matter how he may defame brave men in the process.

On the first day of October, 1914, Mosley was gazetted to the 16th Lancers. That was a normal culmination of his work at Sandhurst, and in normal times he would have derived from it the ordinary pleasure and satisfaction of a subaltern in joining a famous regiment. But for Mosley the appointment held more of heartache and anxiety than of pleasure, for he had secured a cavalry commission at a time when trench-warfare had supervened on the Western Front, and the opinion was being expressed that, apart from a breakthrough in the remote future, the cavalry were likely to rust behind the lines "for the duration." To Mosley, as to all mettlesome young men of the period, the thought of kicking his heels about at the base while his fellow-countrymen went into action was more than abhorrent - it was beyond words calamitous.

He was not the sort of man, however, to sigh away the time in vain regrets. To think with him has always been to act. Looking ahead at probable developments - another of his habits - he came to the conclusion that one of the decisive "Fronts" of the war was certain to be the air, and he saw admirable scope for service in this element. He promptly applied for a job with the Royal Flying Corps. So rapidly did he contrive his transfer that, gazetted to the Lancers in October, 1914, he was flying over the German lines as an observer before the end of that year. Among the first hundred airmen to leave for France, he was one of the very few to survive.

One visualises the young Oswald Mosley of those early days of the war exulting in the thrill and audacity of the planes, deriding danger, defying death; a young Englishman, representative of hundreds of thousands of young Englishmen, inflexible in resolve, conscious of high purposes, and yet not for some time seeming to suspect that the whole business was anything other than a great game that one naturally played desperately hard to win, its whole difference from other games being the hazard of a soldier's grave. He wrote to his mother charging her not to grieve if he should be killed, as he was sure that he would find death "a most interesting experience." It was that spirit in her young men, more than any other psychological factor, that swept Britain forward to victory, even though the lightness of heart in course of time became a little less apparent, and the faces of men confronting the mud-caked and blood-caked agony of the fields of France a good deal more haggard and lined.

Full realisation of the madness which had overtaken the world did not at first penetrate the armour of gaiety which the British troops wore, and continued to wear, no matter how riddled, until the last hour of the war. But the zest and freshness of those early days were never quite recaptured, and by insensible degrees, though the fact was heroically concealed, horror entered into its dominion over men's minds. The youngsters who reached maturity amid the inferno of steel and flame knew what it was to feel within them the pride of manhood as they gave their devoted services through one terrible month after another; but they knew much more - they knew the authentic sufferings of Hell. Tempered by fire as they were, they were in many cases no less certainly torn from their original patterns and cast almost in new moulds. That this happened to Oswald Mosley I believe to be beyond dispute, although in his case Britain is likely to have no cause to lament the change.

In October 1914, he was a brand new cavalry subaltern. His whole ardour was concentrated upon the military life. He had enough money to be able to enjoy it. He was fond of horses and the open air. He had the physique - he was a giant in height and proportionately well-built. He had good looks and charm. He was the cavalry officer par excellence. Possessing an abundance of gifts, he would have risen to high rank. He would perhaps have become a military leader, planning and wining great battles. But that would have been all. He would have remained the cavalry officer, looking at life from the special angle of the cavalry officer, stamped with the consciousness of caste which cavalry officers in particular possess. This line of development the war finally and utterly obliterated.

The war took Mosley by the throat and forced him into an immeasurably more profound conception of life. It made him see the world for the first time as it really was - a bad, stupid place, run by stupid, grasping, and sometimes evil old men. It made him rejoice in the valiant spirit of man, which transcended every barrier of class and creed and revealed itself in these heroic days as common to all men who were spiritually whole. The splendour of the average of the race came to Mosley as a revelation, and at once he saw the shoddy conspiracy of exploitation and snobbishness whereby the average man was excluded from his heritage in the bad world that had so suddenly burst into flames. Like thousands of other men, he became conscious that more than a war was involved; that in that fierce agony a new world was being forged - a world that would one day become fit for the habitation of ordinary decent human beings. And he saw, too, that when the Germans were beaten there would be needed as firm and indomitable a leadership to win through to the new world as any leadership exerted on the field of battle.

The development of Mosley's fine intellect, humanity, and unswerving practical idealism - these things may be traced directly to the metamorphosis which the war wrought in him. We left him however, flying as an observer over the German lines while still a boy of eighteen. As yet the war for him was a thrilling game, and it certainly did not fail to supply him with its thrills. During the winters of '14 and '15 it was almost unknown for a British plane to return from a flight over the German lines without being hit. The engines of that period made low flying essential, so that the targets presented were almost too good to miss. Time after time Mosley nearly lost his life in these adventures, and even such risks do not appear to have been sufficient for him, since he managed to attach himself to the infantry in the second battle of Ypres. Hitherto he had, as it were, looked down on the war, escaping its revolting stenches and other crudities of close-quarter fighting without escaping any of its dangers. Now he was to see it all around him and to smell its odours of death and corruption, to which was added in this battle - for the first time in history - the amiable perfumes of poison gas. He was the last man in Ypres to see the famous Cloth Hall before it was destroyed by shell fire, and made his exit from the doomed town riding on a waggon-load of bombs - by no means the most carefree journey of his life.

Such were the distractions he chose when not engaged in the air, which continued to be his main sphere of activity until he had a crash in France, resulting in injuries to his leg a good deal more serious than was suspected at the time. The damage, was hastily patched up, and Mosley took advantage of the break to train at Shoreham for his pilot's certificate. Soon after he had taken his ticket, his regiment in France - which was doing dismounted service in the line after all - was blown up and decimated by the explosion of a huge mine. In urgent need of every available officer, the 16th Lancers sent out in all directions to recall those who had been temporarily transferred to other units, with the result that Mosley was soon on his way back to France at the head of a draft which he had collected from the Curragh. He went into action with his regiment at Loos, and spent the rest of the winter with them going in and out of the line.

Thus to his experience of war-flying and infantry battles was now added first-hand knowledge of trench warfare, which led to yet another classic experience of that time - hospital. Standing sometimes waist-deep in water during his performance of his trench duties, Mosley's injured leg gave way. It swelled to the size of a bolster. He seems to have tried to conceal the fact, judging by what one of the men who served under him told me - that he caused himself to be carried in and out of the line rather than "go sick." Such grand folly was part and parcel for those days. Fortunately, his condition was eventually spotted by his colonel, who had him packed off, without a moment's delay, to hospital.

Round his bed in England gathered several leading surgeons, who shook their heads over his leg and declared that it had to come off. What such a pronouncement meant to a man of Mosley's intensively active habits can be imagined. Fresh advice was continuously and urgently sought until the father of one of his brother-officers, Watson-Cheyne, agreed to perform an operation that had never been before tried, with the result that after many weary months on crutches, and nearly three years with irons grappling his leg, he gradually regained its use sufficiently, as has been noted, to become a fencer of international repute. Even so, it is still an inch and a half shorter than the other, resulting in a slight limp normally and a pronounced limp after a long march with the young crusaders who were later to gather round him in his great fight for the soul of Britain. The surgeon who performed the operation declared that Mosley was the bravest man he had ever met.

Physical incapacity now ruled out any possibility of his resuming his Army career, even if his new spiritual orientation had not already done so. There was only one way in which he could serve that vision which had come to him, as it had come to millions of other Englishmen, of a world cleansed and purified by fire, and that was the way of political action. Accordingly, while the war was still being waged with relentless fury on the other side of the Channel, Mosley hobbled around Government offices, helping his country to the best of his now limited ability, but, at the same time, obtaining valuable insight into administrative methods, notably at the Ministry of Munitions and the Foreign Office. It seems that he formed a very high opinion of the Civil

Service, for he has often been heard to say that Whitehall has no equals either for integrity or for brains. In his spare time he settled down to an intensive study of political science. Mosley's political thought flowed in three main channels.

First, as has been briefly mentioned, the war discovered for him the average man. Mosley was impressed and inspired by the disinterestedness, the courage, the tenacity, the sheer nobility of ordinary men in the face of every kind of abomination and peril, having seen them fling themselves upon mutilation and death without any knowledge of why they did so except that their country required of them that they should surrender the hope and promise and sweetness of their lives. Mosley was determined - his determination amounted to a passion - that, for his part, he would work unremittingly in the cause of a new social order which would break down existing social barriers by means of which these plain, heroic men and women were repressed and hampered and snubbed, and that he would not rest until there came into being a new economic order to replace the lawless rampage which withheld from them their dues. That was the first of Mosley's aims when he decided to enter the political arena.

His second aim was no less strongly defined. As he had been impressed by the individual efforts of his fellow countrymen in the stress of war, so he had been impressed - and impressed tremendously - by their collective effort. The contribution made by the British Empire towards the common victory filled him with pride as it filled the men of his generation with pride. Before the war the cry of "decadence" had been raised. During the war Britain showed herself, not decadent, but resurgent. Mosley admired the mighty corporate spirit which the Mother Country had put forth: he admired no less the unswerving loyalty of the great Dominions and Colonies overseas, who sent their tall, splendid young men in hundreds of thousands to fight and to die in a quarrel remote from their own shores, impelled by ties of blood and sentiment, but with no material interests to be served. Observing the Imperial peoples in their majesty and their might,

Mosley was convinced that the future lay with them; that the British Empire was more than ever destined to lead the vanguard of the world. He pictured economic planning within the Empire to serve the interests of all, redistribution of population to build up happy colonies wherever there was room for them, steady and sustained help for the daughter-nations because of their great sacrifices, and a community purpose shared by all the people of the Empire and sanctified by the flowing of brave blood on the fields of war. It was Mosley's second resolve to further the cause of Empire by every means in his power, and this aim he joined to the first under the not very satisfactory title of "Socialistic Imperialism" - a title which, nevertheless, conveys clearly enough what he had in mind, and which possesses extraordinary significance in the light of his subsequent career.

His third current thought concerned the actual fact of war, then still in progress. Mosley had seen war for himself; he had suffered from it, and, more important, he had seen the sufferings of others and their deaths. The horror of it, the futility of it, the sickening absurdity and waste of it - these things had struck deep within him. His regard for the military virtue stood higher than ever. He could conceive no more magnificent service than that of men prepared to die for their country should the need arise. But to prevent the need arising, so to order affairs that the hideous madness of European war never again blasted fine men to pieces - that was perhaps Mosley's dominant hope. No man emerged from the war less of a pacifist: no man emerged from it a greater friend of peace. Thus strongly armed with his convictions, Oswald Ernald Mosley embarked upon one of the most vital political quests in the history of the nation. If he had little idea of the storms that lay ahead of him; if he did not dream of the blasts of hatred that he was to inspire, and the whirlpools of fear which gave them birth, then no less certainly he had no notion of the range and potency of the challenge he was to present, on behalf of the British people, to the bad old order that tyrannised over Britain and the civilised world.

3 - *Following Lloyd George*

On July 22, 1918, the members of Harrow Conservative and Unionist Association met to select a candidate for the Division. There were four applicants - two strong local men, one from Headquarters, and a young ex-officer who walked into the room with a limp. He was Oswald Mosley.

Mosley's speech - the first he had ever delivered in public, although nobody suspected the fact - won for him the enthusiastic support of the meeting. "It was a terrific success," wrote one who was present." The President of the Harrow section said that Oswald Mosley's speech 'swept the meeting,' and that there was never a doubt about it afterwards. They were also delighted at his answers to questions. The whole meeting rushed up to him with congratulations, except one man who left in a fury. It was a real triumph." Further opportunities for distinction lay in the immediate future, when the famous "Khaki Election" took place.

Mosley's political objectives when he offered his services to the electors of Harrow were not peculiar to him, but were shared by every decent man and woman in Britain. The stirrings of idealism pervaded the whole atmosphere of the election. It seemed impossible that anybody could wish the world to continue in its pre-war grooves of materialism, humbug and graft. If the war were fought merely to make the world safe for these qualities, then the waging of it was not mere madness, but criminal lunacy of the most satanic kind. Britons felt this with a passionate conviction and were ready to a man, now that the old world lay in ruins about them, to put forward their best efforts, and make further sacrifices, to build a new world - a world more in keeping with human dignity and honour, and more amenable to the requirements of human happiness than the old, whose passing in flames so many of them had miraculously survived.

It was to Mr Lloyd George that they looked for the leadership which the time required. During the war Lloyd George had rescued the nation from the talkers and the ditherers. He had held it together through every kind of ordeal and welded its spirit and its resources into an unconquerable fighting force. He had displayed personal strength and resolution of the rarest order, and this - in combination with his flair for administration, which amounted to genius - entitled him to be regarded more than any other individual, as the man who had led the British people to victory. Lloyd George's incomparable gift for sensing what was in the air left him in no doubt about what was expected of him. He knew that the nation anticipated the building of a new and better order, and he responded in the 1918 Election by calling upon the crusade. He went from one end of the land to the other like a man inspired. His speeches were majestic, touching heights of true sublimity. His fervour was irresistible. The enthusiasm he aroused wherever he went was equalled only by the splendour of his utterances.

Here is a passage from one of his speeches which recalls the spirit of the campaign and the high idealism of the times; "There are many things which are wrong and which ought not to be - poverty, wretchedness and squalor. Let us cleanse this noble land. Let us cleanse it and make it a temple worthy of the sacrifice which has been made for its honour. Let us cleanse the temple of things which dishonour the structure, dishonour the altar, and dishonour the sacrifice made on that altar. Rise to the occasion! Out of the darkness let us see that something is brought up that will warm the hearths of England and lighten and brighten its homes and illuminate the roads along which England shall march to a nobler and grander future."

These thoughts found an echoing response in the speeches of politicians all over the country, and they found something more than an echoing response in the speeches of the young man of twenty-two who was calling the electors of Harrow to the battle.

Young Mosley was an admirer of Lloyd George. He believed in what that leader had done for Britain in the war; he believed, with intense earnestness, in what that leader was destined to do for Britain in the future years of peace. For his own part there was nothing - literally nothing - that he would not have ventured or suffered in order to help Lloyd George in the fulfilment of his vision of a better Britain for the British people.

Mosley's own election addresses and speeches went even a little further - it would have been impossible to go much further - than those of Lloyd George. His challenge to the great vested interests, which spread like an omnivorous vampire over the face of community life, was resonant at the very start of his political career, since he advocated measures for reconstruction which could only be carried out at their expense and in the teeth of their enmity - high wages and shorter hours as the basis of a prosperous home market, public control of electricity and transport, national housing schemes with special safeguards against jerry-building and profiteering, the abolition of slums and back-to-back houses, the compulsory requisition of land for social purposes, educational facilities from the cradle to the university, and far-reaching schemes of health and child-welfare reform. This programme, it should be remembered, was put forward by Mosley as a Conservative supporter of Lloyd George's Coalition. The fact that it did not preclude his adoption by the Harrow Conservative Association does much to explain the atmosphere of the period.

Mosley's choice of the Conservative Party was perhaps inevitable. He was a patriot - and Conservative patriotism had previously been more reliable than Liberal patriotism, and a much stauncher custodian of the Imperial ideal. He had a passionate love of the land - and Conservatism, however, inadequate in its efforts, had at least displayed some concern for the neglected countryside.

He was determined to lend his full weight to secure economic order in place of economic tyranny - and right down through the ages Conservatism had put up a show - even if a disastrously poor show - against the callousness and injustice which attended the rise of economic liberalism throughout the world. Moreover, the Tories had successfully supported Lloyd George during the war, and Mosley saw no reason why they should not support him with equally fortunate results in the great campaigns of peace which were then being prepared.

Although it was as a Conservative-Coalitionist that he entered the arena, a more exact definition of his politics even at that time would have been National Socialist. Mosley's own phrase "Socialistic Imperialism," which he did not hesitate to proclaim to an essentially Tory electorate, implied exactly that. He went so far as to assert that the whole Coalition policy could be contained within that early definition of his aims. "Our policy," he told his audience, "is to blot out the manifold disgraces of our national life as far as any Government can. We have set before you a great social, progressive programme, a great Imperial programme. We must go forward as a great united people, as the greatest people in the world, with all the force behind us of our greatness, our wealth, and our power." On another occasion he affirmed that for him the great desideratum in international as in social problems was "the maximum amount of freedom for the individual without detriment to the interests of the community at large." By way of example, he pointed to the British Empire, "which holds a great trusteeship for humanity in every part of the world."

Readers who have been misled by the lies about Mosley's supposed inconsistency should note these early pronouncements, since they were the keystone of his political aims, from which he has never departed throughout his life.

Mosley's first election was the only relatively peaceful one of his career up to the present time. As yet he was an unknown quantity. He expressed very advanced views about social reform, it is true, but so did many other politicians, and there was nothing to indicate in those early days that a politician had arrived on the scene so grossly heretical as to mean what he said. Fear had still to be born - that fear which was to rise against the young man in a swelling sea of rage.

The fight was quaintly remarkable for the fact that - choice of men apart - there was nothing to fight about. Both Mosley and his opponent - a Mr. A. R. Chamberlayne who described himself as an Independent - were admirers of Lloyd George; both advocated the same programme. Chamberlayne supported Lloyd George in spite of the Coalition; Mosley, being the official candidate, supported him through the Coalition - that was the only difference.

The campaign was consequently innocuous, although Chamberlayne gave his opponent a mild introduction to that kind of election tactics, so dear to democracy, which searches for personal irrelevances wherewith to belabour and belittle the other man. He seized triumphantly upon Mosley's youth - a not very happy choice in 1918. "That bit of a boy," he would say derisively of his opponent. As he himself was over sixty the boomerang did not fail to come back from Mosley in references to "grandfather."

The absurdity of supposing that a boy of eighteen was fit to die for his country, but that a young man of twenty-two was not fit to legislate for his country was duly underlined. "The problems which now confront us demand the qualities of youth, originality, energy, and driving force," said Mosley. "Young men are years older than they were before the war, and they are thinking more. Most of the Members of the House of Commons were too old to fight; and in my view no one can represent the new generation that has fought so well as the men who have been through the same experience, and so have the experience and understanding necessary to the proper solution of the problems of today."

The result of the election was:

| Mosley | 13,959 |
| Chamberlayne | 3,007 |

Something more than Mosley's good looks and eloquence went to the shaping of this result. It cut deeper than that. The people of Harrow, as they were to show in stormier days, had come to trust Mosley as few men have been trusted by electorates. It was a vote for Mosley the man. It was a vote for youth. It was a vote for the future which youth was to build under the inspired leadership of David Lloyd George. That, at least, was the expectation of the time.

Mosley had a presentiment of another kind when he took his seat in Parliament. He went there with great hope, resolved to play a full part in the making of the new world, and conscious of his own awakening powers. His self-confidence was fortunate; without it we should have heard no more of him - he would have been submerged in the seas of nonentity in which so many political aspirants have been lost on arriving at Westminster.

To say that Oswald Mosley was appalled when he looked around him at the faces of his fellow-legislators would be too mild a term. He had not expected to find an assembly of cherubim. But neither had he dreamed that the Parliamentary physiognomy would prove so lacking in every quality of aspiration and endeavour. He saw on every side small, dried-up men with mean faces; big pompous, pot-bellied men with smug faces; there were thin, spiteful mouths and heavy, selfish mouths; there were yellow skins and flaccid skins; and in almost every eye there was the glint of egotism and greed. These were Mr. Lloyd George's soldiers of peace; the men entrusted with the "cleansing of the temple"; the crusaders on behalf of the new age which was to be built upon the agony of youth. Mosley saw them as they were - a Parliament mostly of profiteers and opportunists, assembled not to further the cause of the new world but to patch up and conserve the ugly old world which had brought them great wealth in the past, and which would bring them still greater wealth in the future as long as they retained the reins of power.

These, many of them, were the jackals who had grown fat on the sacrifice of brave men, and who had sensed further opportunity for carousal upon the gains of peace which the brave men brought. These were the hard-boiled materialists who drove Lloyd George onto the reparations ramp, from which they hoped to derive further profits from the stricken people of Germany; who urged him to the crimes of Versailles, who swept him headlong into every disaster of a most disastrous Ministry. The hopes and faiths of the war period, the idealism of the war's aftermath - none of these things had impinged upon their minds. Mosley knew that by looking at them.

This was the assembly that came to be known as "The Hard-Faced Parliament," the assembly which made of Mr. Lloyd George's crusade one of the most lamentable fiascos of modern times. Lloyd George was not altogether to blame for this gigantic betrayal, although it will always stand to the debit side of his ledger. He was, we must remember, a party politician, and had been for over thirty years. The duty of a party politician is to achieve office and keep himself there. That is the tradition of a parliamentary system which has long existed to serve the careers of parliamentarians, and through them, the owners of economic power. Always, in every fundamental conflict of interests, the national interest - the welfare of the people of Britain - has been surrendered to political opportunism and financial greed. That is the essence of Liberalism; the creed which insists that absolute freedom must be granted to any anti-social minority that wishes to organise for private plunder at the expense of the masses.

When Lloyd George was making his magnificent speeches during the election he was, no doubt, sincere enough, being carried away by his own eloquence if nothing else. One imagines that he would have liked to have cleansed the temple of Britain's national life and made it a memorial worthy of the sacrifice of a million dead. But when the thunder of the elections and the shouting were over, and the realities of the position had to be approached in cold blood, he found that the forces arrayed against the new order were too strong for him to attempt the assault. The first move in this direction would have led the profiteers to hurl him from office. Financial houses would have arranged for a money-panic; the bought Press would have been unleashed. Political crises of the gravest kind would have been manufactured in order to encompass his defeat. What was needed was a new man and a new movement, with an entirely new concept of political method - a man and a movement dauntless enough and disciplined enough to dare the vested interests in all their entrenchments, to grapple with them and subdue them and force them to serve the national interest. Lloyd George was not the right man for this job, and neither was his movement the right movement, since - Heaven help it! - it consisted almost exclusively of the enemy.

What is more, the Prime Minister had grown up in a world where politics and economic power had always gone hand in hand, with the result that he was himself too deeply compromised with the existing order to be able to put up a show against it. The big financiers of the age were his intimates; the captains of industry and commerce his firm friends. The crusade, therefore, collapsed before it can justly be said to have started, and Lloyd George settled down to temporise and make his peace with the individualists, from several of whom he accepted large sums for his Party funds in return for peerages and baronetcies and knighthoods. Expediency thus triumphed over idealism, and still continues to do so long after Mr. Lloyd George's old followers have tired of Mr. Lloyd George's gifts and exchanged him for Mr. Baldwin, who has none.

Among the members of the 1918 Parliament, however, there was a large sprinkling of men whose intentions were admirable. These men had not looked upon their pledges as so many pieces of election machinery to be scrapped immediately after their return. They wanted something done, something which, in Mr. Lloyd George's flashing phrase, would illuminate the roads of England's march to a nobler and grander future. There were about one hundred and fifty such members at the outset, and upon them rested whatever hope there was of attaining to that future within a measurable space of time. To protect and further their aims they formed themselves into an organisation known as the "New Members' Association." Their purpose was to force through Parliament all those measures of reform, all those great plans for social justice and an economic square deal, which constituted the programme upon which they had secured election to the House.

Their secretary and animating spirit was a young man of twenty-two returned for Harrow, whom the stunt newspapers had already introduced to the general public as "The Commons Baby." This particular baby the Commons were to find quite remarkably difficult, and, indeed, politically impossible, to rear in the way it should go.

4 - The First Challenge

Mosley was now to see the democratic method revealed in its inherent weakness as a means of furthering national welfare, and its pliable strength as an instrument of humbug and oppression with which vested interests made secure their profits at the expense of the people.

No sooner had the "New Members' Association" caused its presence to be felt in the House than the Old Guard decided that it had to be destroyed. It mobilised its special storm troops for the purpose: the first wave of which was composed of its less grim-looking individuals, who crawled to the assault armed only with bland, ingratiating smiles. They came amongst the new members, insinuated themselves into their good graces, flattered them, whispered to them that assuredly such brilliant young men could only be destined for brilliant careers culminating in many a high office of state, and generally led them up the political garden path in many different directions at once. The youngsters whom they button-holed in the lobby and took out to lunch were not ordinarily men of weak character. Most of them had fought for their country, many with distinction. But they had not the slightest inkling of the truth - neglected by democracy - that discipline and leadership are as essential in a political crusade as in a military campaign. Had this realisation come to them the history of the post-war period might have made more pleasant reading. As it was they were inexperienced; they allowed their crafty elders to sow suspicion and dissention in their ranks; they succumbed to the blandishments so skilfully bestowed on them and went over to the enemy in large batches until there was only one small group left to carry on the fight and hold high the torch flung to them by the men who died in battle. This group stood together for a time, and then its members also began to go the diverse ways of the ten little nigger boys, so that in the end for all practical purposes only one man of all Lloyd George's Coalitionists was found sticking to his post, resolved that the vision should not perish and lashing the Government day after day, night after night, for its cowardly capitulation to vested interests and its ghastly betrayal of the nation's cause. That man was Oswald Mosley - the "Commons' Baby."

Mosley had material to spare for his attacks, not only because of what the Government failed to do, but because of what he did. The Treaty of Versailles horrified him with its ineptitude. He saw that there could be no prospect of a saner order built upon so lamentably mean and rickety a foundation. At home the money-grabbers were busy smashing down the restrictions imposed by Government after the nation had been impoverished through inordinate profiteering on war materials, and evincing a determination that henceforward the world should be placed unreservedly at their disposal for plunder. There was also the scrapping of the entire national machinery set up for production during the war, which disgusted Mosley, both on its own account and because of the first-class ramp which accompanied it. Plant was sold to the Government's favourite profiteers at knock-down prices. Surplus material worth millions of pounds was thrown in without the small formality of payment being demanded of the profiteers. Plant all over the world was sold without even having been valued. Such was the first part of the superstructure of Mr. Lloyd George's land fit for heroes. Then there was the House-Subsidy Act which, introduced to aid the working-man, in many instances ended in a jerry-builders' racket at the expense of the working-man. There were the recurring scandals of coxcombs buying titles for themselves in return for contributions to Mr. Lloyd George's party fund. There was the squandering of £100,000,000 on the futile Russian adventure. There was the no less extravagant folly of the Mesopotamian expenditure to please the oil kings - "squandering money on desert sands." There was the equanimity with which Lloyd George allowed his unemployment scheme, embodied in a Labour Bill, to be twice thrown out by his own henchmen. There was the duping of the miners over the Sankey Report, which had offered a real opportunity for reorganisation in the coal industry. There was the business of Chanak, when Lloyd George and Churchill invited another war with Turkey and made the British Empire ridiculous. And there was the mounting folly of the Government's Irish Policy, calculated to estrange Irishmen forever by the substitution of irregular and undisciplined Black and Tans for the Regular Army.

It has been said that Mosley broke with the Coalition over the Irish question, but that is not altogether accurate. His quarrel was based upon the Government's policy of betrayal as a whole. Nevertheless, his views on Ireland were sharply defined. In the summer of 1920, before Sinn Fein had begun to organise its final series of outrages and the Government to repay those outrages in kind, Mosley advocated peace on a Dominion basis with the elected representatives of the Irish. If peace had been made at that time, in an atmosphere of generosity and sound sense, it is probable that Ireland would have become a less equivocal member of the British Commonwealth. But the Government scornfully rejected Mosley's plan only to be coerced back to it two years later after they had let loose the Black and Tans and created an intensified hatred of this country in the breasts of Irishmen throughout the world.

Several months before this came to pass Mosley had given Britain one of its few glimpses of a Member of Parliament standing by his principles. In the autumn of 1920 he severed his connection with Lloyd George and crossed the floor of the House. This was the signal for the first big political storm to burst upon him. So long as he had criticised the Government from the Government benches his colleagues had suffered him with a tolerance which just managed to conceal their fear and mistrust of him as a new and dangerous force in British politics. They ascribed his steadfastness to the folly of youth, and told each other that he would find his level in due course. Some were even good enough to predict that the level would be a high one and, indeed, had he continued with the Conservative Party, and cultivated the art of acquiescence according to time-honoured precedents, he would almost certainly have found in the not distant future a political level as high as any in the land. That was the general opinion of accomplished observers at the time, and even after his split with the old parties the newspapers for long continued to refer to him as possessing the stuff of which Prime Ministers are made - a significant estimate, if not a very striking compliment to Mosley.

He had made it clear by his break, however, that in any choice between expediency and principle he would stand by principle - an intolerable heresy. Having tried, and failed, to flatter him into compliance in the early days of the "New Members' Association," the old parties now felt that the position was sufficiently clear to launch upon him the second wave of the democratic assault, which consists of vitriolic abuse, misrepresentation, ridicule, and the sheer weight of concentrated mass denunciation. The hard-faced men had howled when he crossed the floor, but all the jackals of Africa could not have equalled the howls that they gave whenever he rose to speak on the other side, where he had taken his seat as an Independent on the Socialist benches.

Mosley was astounded at the demonstration. He did not realise to what extent he had come to be regarded as a portent by the selfish old men who feared for their wealth, their careers, and their "class." He paid the price for what was considered to be the "betrayal" of that class. When he good-naturedly expressed his surprise at these violent outbursts he was howled at all the more. Since he was not for sale, then clearly he had to be overwhelmed by the loudest vocal barrage which his opponents could produce. This laughable conspiracy of silly old men to shout down the "Commons' Baby" produced an excellent result. It turned Mosley, already a brilliant orator, into a cut-and-thrust debater of ferocity and skill. It sharpened his wit to razor point. It gave an edge to his gift for satire which he used unmercifully upon his foes. Only by holding them up to ridicule and scorn was he able, for many years, to command a hearing in the House.

It is not to be supposed that Mosley, in this great fight against vested interests and political poltroonery, enjoyed these rancorous enmities and outbursts of hooliganism which they brought against him through one Parliamentary period after another. No man is less insensitive than Mosley. His sensibilities are as highly developed as his courage and his brains. There is no great fun for a serious-minded patriot in rising time and again to subdue by invective derisive howls from hundreds of men intolerant of pleas for the welfare of the British nation. Looking back on that time Mosley says that he has no cause to regret the ordeal. "Having survived it I do not regret it," he affirms. Mosley was not overwhelmed, but fortified, because of the matchless spirit that had led him as a child to conquer his dread of horses and which in France had sustained him in the trenches when his leg was swollen to three times its normal size. Throughout the great political battles of his life Mosley's spirit has been proved heroic in the best and highest sense of the word, and never more so than during this prolonged period when, as a very young man, he battled for his ideals against the parliamentary conspiracy to deny him a hearing to speak on behalf of his constituents and of the nation which he served.

The implacability of Mosley's opposition to national misgovernment should not lead us to picture him in those days, or at any other period of his career, as a turbulent fanatic, thriving only in an atmosphere of storm. His mind is essentially constructive, and if this fact did not become popularly known during his first ten years in Parliament, the reason is simply that Parliament has no use for constructive thought and does its best to protect itself against it. Moreover, Mosley's wide culture, his keen sense of humour, and the depth of his passion for life have all helped to keep him from cultivating the disposition of a Robespierre. If these qualities had been unable to prevent him being soured by the darkness of his political disillusionment one may be sure that his wife would have done so, since in 1920 he married one of the finest and sweetest women of the age, Cynthia Curzon, daughter of the late Marquis Curzon of Kedlestone. Opponents were later to take full advantage of the fact that the wedding was a royal affair, being held in the Savoy Chapel and attended by King George and Queen Mary and by the King and Queen of the Belgians. Cynthia Mosley never faltered in the devoted service she gave to her husband's ideals, and throughout her lamentably short life she was always at his side, a resolute fighter, an inspiring companion, and a dauntless and incorruptible spirit, whose services to her country live on in her husband's work, which she had made her own.

Mosley, as I have said, took his seat as an Independent on the Socialistic benches, and the query will have arisen in the reader's mind as to why he did not join up at once with the Socialists. The answer may be briefly given: the Labour Party repelled him. He thought it a betrayal to work with them. The equivocal attitude of many of its leaders while Britain was fighting for her life disgusted him. He was revolted by its parrot-cries and clichés. He abominated its insistence on the class-war, exactly as he had abominated the same doctrine implicitly promoted from the other side by the men he had just left. Besides, party labels had come to mean so little, the whole game was so empty and shallow, that Mosley was convinced that fresh political alignments would necessarily take place in the near future - alignments with some relation to reality. Therefore, as he told the electors of Harrow, he had no option but to work independently until he saw precisely the form which the new divisions were to take. Mosley thus rather misjudged the situation, not even then being fully aware of the tenacity of the old party system or its power to devitalise and corrupt to the purposes of a lawless capitalism new men and new movements as they advanced to power.

The new alignment has not taken place in the year 1936, and it is not likely to take place until Oswald Mosley's own movement captures Parliament, to force the only division that today has any validity - the division between those who are for Britain and those who are only for themselves.

As the election of 1922 drew near, it was to be expected that the Conservative Central Office should begin to pull strings out at Harrow to make things awkward for its rebellious young ex-member. In July of that year the newspapers reported that the Harrow Division of the Conservative and Unionist Association were taking into serious consideration the independent attitude shown by Mosley, and in the same month the Association announced, in effect, that if he wanted its continued support he would have to say "Yea" or "Nay" exactly as he was bidden by the Party chiefs. This was the wording of its resolution:-

"Any candidate seeking to represent the Harrow Division at the next election in Parliament in the Conservative and Unionist interest, must, as a condition of receiving the support of this Association, pledge himself, if the next General Election results in the formation of a National Unionist Administration, to give that Administration his loyal support. In any event, he must, as a general rule, follow the National Unionist Whip in the Division-Lobby, and if unable to do so in important matters, he must take the Association into his confidence, explaining his reasons and seeking its continued support."

Mosley's reply was withering. He had already brought to a high state of development his gift for tearing absurdities to shreds in a few terse sentences. In the reply he said:-

"This resolution would tie me hand and foot as a servile adherent of the present Coalition Government, whose shallow opportunism and grave mistakes have now been exposed by events that have justified in full measure the opposing policy which I have consistently advanced. It is, therefore, evident that I cannot accept these conditions without a complete reversal of the political position which I have long maintained and which the Association has hitherto supported. No candidate would bind himself in advance to a situation which has not yet arisen, to support leaders who are not yet even designated in a policy which has not yet been disclosed. A gramophone would be more suitable to these requirements than a human being." He concluded his letter with the following clear-cut statement of principle:-

"No fear for my own political fortunes will deflect me from a policy which I believe to be essential to the welfare of our country, and I shall certainly submit the issue to the verdict of the electorate.... I pledged myself only to support the Coalition in the policy contained in its election manifesto, and outside the limits of that programme I hold myself absolutely free to deal with new issues as they arise."

At the same time, he gave the electors of Harrow reasons for his breach with the Government, some of which have already been noted. Among them were: profligate extravagance; the pouring of money on the sands of Mesopotamia; the squandering of money on an inflated bureaucracy; the refusal to countenance withdrawal from costly enterprises abroad or to concentrate on building up a better national life at home.

The result was the withdrawal of official Tory support and a decision to fight Mosley at the impending election. They chose as his opponent a Major Charles Ward Jackson, and extraordinary efforts were made by them to ensure the defeat of the rebel, in order that others tempted to follow his example might ponder upon the hardness of the lot of the political transgressor who insists upon doing his own thinking.

Major Ward Jackson, who had presumably taken the required pledge to say "Yes" and "No" as he was told by the Whip, did not commit his predecessor's error of referring to his opponent as "that bit of a boy." Instead, he made a worse blunder of his own, affirming - on Heaven knows what authority - that Mosley had incited Indians to revolt against the British Raj. Now Mosley has never suffered electors to be misled by lies told about him wherever it has been possible to nail them down and bring to book those who utter them. He promptly issued a writ for slander against his opponent. Each candidate announced in the local Press that if he was elected, and the action went against him, he would resign his seat. The case was settled, however, by Major Jackson admitting that he had made a mistake and offering a full apology.

Mosley's speeches at this election show that some of his more permanent political views were already in the process of formation. He defined the function of the State, for instance, as "keeping the ring for the consumer" whereas the function of every Government since the beginning of the Industrial Revolution has been to keep the ring for big-scale capitalism. Another important statement, showing that as long ago as 1922 his mind was occupied with the germs of the corporate organisation of industry, was expressed in these words: "A taunt, which is productive of much unrest, that Labour is a mere chattel on the market, should be met by a frank invitation to Labour to participate as a partner with a voice in the destinies of industries to which it devotes its life. Such measures are compatible with the preservation of that individual initiative on which our industries rest, and, at the same time, would go far toward seeing the co-operation of Labour on a basis of joint interest and common humanity."

In 1922, as still more emphatically in 1936, he set his face against disastrous interference in affairs outside our own Imperial concern, warning Britain against the return to the balance of power with its division of Europe into armed camps awaiting their opportunity for attack, and advocating a general withdrawal to the normal bounds of Empire. Above all, he demanded a higher wage system in order to build up the home market, whereas the execrable economics of financial capitalism were even then driving employers towards the disaster of wholesale wage cutting, still further to reduce the purchasing power available to absorb the products of industry.

There was nothing in Mosley's policy to commend itself to Conservatism, and even had it been otherwise, his independence in Parliament and his subsequent explicit refusal to be a puppet on a string was sufficient to start the official machine in motion against him. There would have been little cause for surprise in the circumstances if he had been defeated, but instead, he secured a resounding personal victory over the Party machine.

The figures were:-

Mosley	15,290
Ward Jackson	7,868
Majority	7,422

The victorious rebel went back, fortified, to the battle.

5 - *Independent Sniping*

The 1922 Election put an end to Lloyd George as an executive force in British politics. His Coalition had been smashed by the Tories under Bonar Law and good, honest, Stanley Baldwin, and he now packed up his party money-bags (that million-pound "Fighting Fund") and left Downing Street to marshal from afar armies that were largely non-existent, in what was to become the best Haile Selassie manner. Meanwhile, his successors settled down to the formulation of policies still more dangerous and inept.

Mosley's triumph over the otherwise victorious Tories had done nothing to increase their love of him. Only the emotional outlets of Parliamentary debate, Press denunciation, and platform oratory prevented them choking at the mention of his name, and no opportunity to make full use of these channels was ignored. The politicians vied with the cartoonists to present him in a fantastic light and kill him with ridicule. At the same time they paid him the highest tribute by filling the House whenever he spoke - a kind of political masochism in that he never failed to thrash them with his biting invective. That Mosley was a big man they would strenuously deny, but the crowded audiences which they provided for him in the Commons, together with the sheer violence of their caricature, belied their campaign of belittlement. Moreover, it could not be concealed from the country at large that in the battle of wits this remarkable young man more than held his own against the formidable array of his opponents.

Mosley by this time had a reputation. His deadly attacks against the Coalition Government were well remembered; in particular his description of the Olympian Editor of *The Observer* as a musical doormat which played "See the Conquering Hero Comes" whenever Mr. Lloyd George wiped his boots upon it.

He now pursued the Coalition beyond its grave, asserting that it had followed the most fatal of all policies by doing enough to irritate everybody and not enough to achieve anything. He summed up its adventure in the Near East as "the philanthropic policy of backing both sides - England backing the Greeks and France backing the Turks like a couple of money-making promoters of a prize fight." He predicted humiliation for Britain then, exactly as he was many years later to predict humiliation for Britain over the still more feckless sanctions issue, and the following observation made in those early days is the more interesting on that account: "There is nothing in the world so detrimental to national prestige as being full of bluff and bluster until you get into difficulties and then having to climb down. It is possible to walk downstairs of one's own free will with grace and dignity. It is impossible to be kicked downstairs either with grace or dignity."

Mosley's volleys into the foreign policy of the Conservative administration were no less devastating. He deplored its zeal for futile international mischief-making on principle and even more because of the weaknesses, doubts, and hesitancies with which its interventions were carried out. Sympathising with a British Minister who had been reproached with a lack of firmness in his utterances at Geneva, Mosley asked: "How is it possible to express a perpetual wobble in firm language? Why does not the Minister go to Geneva and there erect a more stately and stable edifice? What is his foundation for the edifice? His foundation is the English Cabinet and their policy. You might as well ask him to build a pyramid upon a jelly-fish." Readers who carry their minds forward to the activities of the British Government fourteen years later will no doubt reflect upon the fact that there is one technique which British statesmen have perfected during the interval - the technique of what Mosley calls the "wobble."

It must not be imagined, however, that his speeches were composed solely of taunts. Always there was evidence of a constructive mind at work, and of a very high devotion to principle, as was shown in the later stages of his "wobble" speech when he made an impassioned plea for the formation of a courageous policy worthy of the grandest traditions of British statesmanship in the past - a policy forged by Britain and not "dragged forever at the chariot wheels of France." That last statement indicates another truth about Mosley. As he represented in himself the aspiration of the millions of men who fought in the War, so was he typical of them in the decency of his attitude towards a foe honourably defeated on the battlefield. There had been no snarling littleness towards each other in the minds of the combatants; that was the fighting spirit of hysterical politicians, frightened profiteers, and the more debased sections of the Press. In the capitulation of Lloyd George to the old order the hysterical attitude triumphed over the heroic, and continues to triumph even at the present time, with the result that British support has always been forthcoming for French schemes of encirclement, leading to the adoption of a mean-spirited, neurotic, and fundamentally ungenerous treatment of the great German nation. This spirit always filled Mosley with disgust, and time after time he assailed it, demanding in the words of a great poet, a policy of "honour and of English things." When the French marched into the Ruhr, more or less with Tory blessings, Mosley's anger leapt out time after time at the revolting old men who were systematically destroying the magnificent values which alone had lent balance and redress to the madness of the War, and when it became clear that the French had chosen black troops to let loose among German women, his indignation mounted to heights of passion rarely reached in the House, as for instance, his declaration, amidst cheers even from the foe: "Some party has got to break this death-grapple of civilisation in which top-dog and under-dog are bleeding to death. Towards France let us end this sycophantic adulation punctuated with snarls."

Such a man could not be ignored or dismissed with a sneer. The better type of thinker and publicist began to follow his career with interest. A measure of justice was even accorded him by some of the newspapers. The *Sunday Express* wrote of one of his speeches on Mesopotamia that it was "like a light shining in a dark House of Commons." Commenting on the same effort the late T.P. O'Connor wrote: "Young Oswald Mosley made an excellent speech. I was very much afraid that his courage and his violent differences with his own party would have driven him out of the representation of so respectable a Tory constituency as Harrow, but he won on a huge majority - a tribute to courageous honesty one does not see too often in British politics." Another journal stated: "Mr. Mosley has been tipped as a future Prime Minister." On another occasion the *Sunday Express* wrote: "He has a daring mind, any amount of courage, and is a master of glib and biting sarcasm. Before he is thirty-five he is likely to count for a great deal in British politics, unless he becomes a second Lord Hugh Cecil. That is his only danger." The *Sunday Express* may care to observe that the danger is now past! Then there was the *Daily News*, which referred to his "intense passion for social justice"; *Reynolds News*, which found an admirable testimony to his qualities in the hatred borne him by the Tories; and the *Westminster Gazette*, which paid him many fine tributes, of which I select two: "He has the qualifications of a first-rate debater - courage and coolness, an excellent command of English and a quick wit," and "Although in his twenty-seventh year Mr. Mosley is spoken of by old and experienced Parliamentary hands as composed of the stuff of which Prime Ministers are made. The most polished literary speaker in the Commons, words flow from him in graceful, epigrammatic phrases that have a sting in them for the Government and the Conservatives. Yet all the while he smiles pleasantly. To listen to him is an education in the English language, also in the art of delicate but deadly repartee."

Thus did Mosley make his mark, not only for what he said, but for the consummate art with which he said it. The *New Statesman* on this score was particularly interesting, and not alone because of its subsequent shrill screams against him: "Mr. Mosley is training himself into the position of the most literary speaker in the Commons. His arrows are always barbed and often subtly aimed. He has courage and cares nothing for rebuffs, and his mind shows both distinction and elevation." The words "training himself" were perhaps more literally true than the journal realised. Incredible as it may seem to those who know only the Mosley of the present day there was a time when his voice was often betrayed into a high-pitched note, which in the view of many people was a big handicap to his delivery. He seems to have shared this opinion, but instead of accepting the handicap he set to work, with that forthright determination, which is typical of the man, to eradicate the defect and obtain complete mastery over his vocal chords. He subjected himself for many months to the discipline of voice production at the hands of an expert, so that today the thought of this early defect seems grotesque, such is the controlled power and majestic quality of his diction.

Mosley's time was occupied during this second Parliamentary period in attacking the Government for its futility at home and abroad, in making known his views about the evil of indirect taxation, and in performing one or two signal services for his constituents. Nevertheless he was not satisfied with the sphere in which his work was set. As an Independent he felt his position to be a barren one. There was little that a political freelance, without a movement, without political affiliations of any kind, could achieve in the way of constructive action. Even destructive action was limited in scope. Sustained sniping activities were all very well, but what was needed to dislodge the enemy was an artillery barrage of a magnitude impossible for any one man to supply.

The country was full of speculation as to which party Mosley would join, and absurd rumours went the rounds and were duly blazoned in the Press, even the nonsense that he was to be elevated to the House of Lords. There is no doubt that the Liberal Party were anxious to enlist his services in their cause: his forensic attack would have been worth all of Lloyd George's "Fighting Fund," at any rate judging by the use they made of it. They tried every form of flattery, foolishly imagining that their projected recruit was to be won by honeyed words. It was a waste of time, because Mosley had an ingrained loathing of Liberal economics and its accompanying political humbug. On the other hand members of the Labour Party were entertaining a similar hope, except a few leaders who feared to be outshone by so formidable a recruit. The Tory Press was now making much use of the phrase "Mosley's socialistic leanings." He was described in a Labour paper as a guild-socialist. The *Morning Post* remarked with humour that for some time his speeches has resembled the final sermons of a young Anglican parson before going over to Rome. But Mosley, still awaiting that new alignment of parties which he believed to be essential before reality could be imported into politics, said nothing about his plans, although his action in speaking on a Socialist's platform brought around him a continual buzz of reporters demanding information as to whether or not his intentions towards that Party were honourable.

At this time both Mosley and his secretary, George Sutton, experienced modern journalism in all the fullness of its flavour. An evening paper reporter called to see Mosley, who was out. He thereupon engaged Sutton in an informal political discussion, and Sutton made various observations about the general situation, giving expression to his own personal views. After an hour's friendly conversation the reporter went his way, assuring Sutton that he would of course, treat what he had said as confidential. One can imagine the horror of both Mosley and his secretary when the evening paper came out with a "splash" story in which Sutton's remarks were set forth almost word for word and ascribed to Mosley in a special interview the reporter claimed to have had with him. Sutton emerged from that encounter a wiser man.

The year 1923 brought another election, and Mosley again entered his candidature for the Harrow Division. This time the issue was "Protection." The mounting unemployment figures, due to lack of Government policy strengthened the demand of industrialists for protection, and the Tory administration decided to try out certain milk-and-water measures which would have the majority of free-trade interests unaffected. Mosley opposed protection, which may surprise readers when they come to examine his present uncompromising economic proposals as set out in a later chapter. Yet there has been very little inconsistency in his attitude. He fought against protection because it was, and remains, one of those half-measures which are more dangerous than no measure at all. Mosley knew that there was no possibility of Britain's economic life being reorganised to build up a home market through a controlled increase in the purchasing power of the people; that protection did not so much exclude goods as make them dearer through the creation of monopoly conditions; and that the result could only be a further decrease in consumption, whereas the crying need of the country was for an expansion of the power to consume. Protection in the hands of Parliamentary democracy, moreover, has since proved itself a futile and sometimes a corrupt instrument for almost every purpose, in that the industrialists use it largely as a shield to stave off the effects of their own laziness, incompetence, and failure to organise in accordance with modern needs. Mosley had a premonition that its introduction would prove to be beneficial mainly to the profiteers, and he opposed it with vigour. "Is there any chance," he asked, "that wages will rise to correspond to prices? They will be kept down, there will be more unemployment and the wage-earning classes will be at the mercy of monopolistic industrialists." Events have shown him to be right. At the same time he insisted that there was no Free Trade doctrinaire. The truth is that his mind had already begun to evolve what was to become his famous policy of economic insulation, but not for many years, until he had thought all round the problem, did he present this solution for the consideration of the British people.

The election at Harrow was not so unpleasant as the previous one, although unpleasantness did creep in. The Tory nominee - a Mr. Hugh Morris, who had achieved some distinction as a debater at the Cambridge Union - announced at his first meeting that he proposed to fight without recourse to "personalities," but that ideal proved a little too high for his attainment. The atmosphere was not improved by the appearance on his platform of a ministerial "big-gun" in the person of Mr. L.C.M. Amery who used the occasion to attack Mosley along familiar democratic lines. Although the Coalition and Tory Governments had betrayed every one of their election promises, and although it was on this ground that Mosley had severed his connection with them, Amery did not blush to lay the charge of inconsistency and betrayal at his door - a charge which the intellectually dishonest, for want of a more convincing lie, repeat with increasing vehemence at the present time. "Bolshevist" was another amiable description Amery found for him. Mosley has never suffered himself to be blackguarded by his opponents without a suitable reply, and his description of Amery went straight to the man's weakness, which expressed itself in that particular brand of Imperialism which is all froth and moonshine, barren of any sense of Imperial aspiration. He counter-attacked at his next meeting, therefore, and delighted the audience by declaring - "Mr. Amery has presented me in the phrase of 'a Bolshevist.' When I hear this man, who has been responsible for so many futile adventures, with his loud and rancorous shout in place of argument 'Yah Bolshevist,' I am not greatly disconcerted by this busy, but ineffective, little drummer-boy in the Jingo brass band." So Amery got no change out of that encounter.

Between the two election periods the Conservatives had worked without ceasing to recapture the seat and revenge themselves upon the rebel who had flouted and beaten them. Their protection policy, moreover, was calculated to appeal to a middle-class constituency whose industrial shares had plunged into seemingly bottomless disaster and who would be likely to welcome almost any promise of a quick restorative. The Tory method was to try to invoke for their own advantage the lofty patriotism of the war years. "Keep the Home Fires Burning" was their slogan, which led to Mosley's contemptuous criticism: "They ask you to keep the home fires burning. They have been kept burning by the Conservatives; they are the fires of degradation and anguish which are eating out the heart of our people. They ask you to keep the home fires burning. I ask you to put out the fires of misery, and light in our people once again the flame of progress and great ambition, and by that shall we win through to triumph over the disastrous winters that threaten us." His last words to the electors were: "I appeal to you to reject with derision and contempt a policy which is the last gambler's throw of a bankrupt and discredited party."

One factor which did Mosley a good deal of harm in this predominantly Tory district was his refusal to allow himself to be described as an "Independent Conservative." He was now convinced that no progress, no enlightenment, no human value of any kind could usefully be sought in Conservatism, and to newspapers which erred in their description of him he promptly wrote avowing himself "an unremitting opponent of any Conservative administration." Many votes were lost by this attitude, but his principle remained unequivocal and clear.

The result was:-

Mosley	14,079
Morris	9,433
Majority	4,646

Although the majority was reduced, the unceasing Tory campaign against him in the constituency during many months made this victory even more triumphant than the previous one.

As a result of the election the balance of power was soon to enable the Labour Party for the first time to occupy the seat of Government.

6 - Society Is Shocked

Mosley watched the Labour Party in office with close interest. During its long bid for power its propaganda had advocated almost every kind of national and imperial disruption. It had spoken a political language new to our shores and evinced a spirit which seemed hostile to the tradition of our people and their immemorial way of life. The landscape, embracing that sense of native land which has developed during a thousand years of unbroken historical continuity, found no place in its philosophy; the new men, when they thought about it all, regarded landscape, grotesquely, as a sort of capitalist possession, and its language, the language of patriotism, as no more than the voice of capitalist exploitation. Therefore the inhabitants of this country were not to think of themselves as Britons but as workers - not as workers of Britain, but as workers of the world.

As workers of the world they were summoned to unite. Mosley, like every other patriot with a deep feeling for his native soil and tradition, loathed this concept with its laborious manufacture of shoddy, synthetic values and its overthrow of the whole of the past, good and bad alike, to make way for the fashioning of life according to theories that had in their utterance a hollow, metallic ring and reflected nothing of the enduring qualities of the human heart and soul - no love of country, no sense of nationhood or of national values forged upon the anvils of common history and of dangers shared, no poetry, no music, no laughter. Nobody saw more clearly than Mosley the necessity of revolutionary economic changes if Britain was to live, but to dress his ideas in these rags of cosmopolitanism would have done them as much justice as would be done to the English beauty of a Shakespearian play translated into Esperanto and acted by stuttering Levantine Jews.

Leaders of the Labour Party had often spoken with wild extravagance of what they proposed to do when opportunity came their way: there had been talk of red revolt and ruthless destruction of many things which Britons hold dear, not excluding, on occasion, equivocal statements about the future position of the Royal Family. Against any such threat Mosley - like millions of his fellow countrymen - would have offered more than political resistance. At the same time, he could not fail to sympathise with that great urge for social betterment which had given the Labour Party its impetus, or fail to admire the spirit of devotion and self-sacrifice which animated so many of its rank and file. He was very much aware, too, that, except for the assistance of a few grand men of the calibre of the late Lord Henry Cavendish Bentinck, Parliamentary support for his views had come entirely from Labour members.

Had Labour in office shown the slightest disposition to implement the purely disruptive part of their policy as outlined in much of their propaganda, Mosley's attitude would not have been in doubt, but since no such disposition was revealed by the 1923 Government, and since it was fighting for its existence against his own foes, the great tyrannical vested interests, he decided that to refuse his co-operation would be to bind himself hand-and-foot to mere prejudice and condemn himself to the indefinite prolongation of an independence which he felt to be sterile. He saw - by this time with much vividness - that the real enemies of the British people were the powerful minority interests wielding the money-weapon, and that the battle against this concealed dictatorship was the most vital of the age. To fight them without allies was quixotic. Mosley decided to join up with Labour and press forwards towards the fulfilment of his ideals in the company of men pledged to the better ordering of the national life. In April 1924, he wrote to Ramsay MacDonald announcing his intention, pointing out that for some time past he had found himself in agreement both with the immediate policy and the ultimate ideals of Labour, and that he had joined in resisting the attacks upon it delivered by a variety of opponents. "In these circumstances," he wrote, "it appears that my proper course is to apply for formal membership of the Labour Party." Mosley's move had long been predicted but this did not rob it of sensation. The outcry was terrific. In the Commons the Tories intensified their barrage of snarls and jeers. The Tory Press published attack after attack, in which his motives were distorted and his sincerity ridiculed and denied. His foes, following Amery's line at Harrow, represented him, in defiance of every fact, as an irresponsible careerist and adventurer. This was all the more ludicrous and dishonest in that, had these things been true, Mosley would unquestionably have stayed with the Conservatives and played the party game for the dominant interests behind the scenes. He had independent means, influential connections, which included the British Foreign Minister, every exterior advantage to carry him to the highest positions in the land along the Tory royal road. The deliberate sacrifice of these advantages to high principle and consistency of ideal stands as a symbol of his honesty, and gives the lie direct to his detractors.

Another result of his new allegiance was not unforeseen, either by Mosley or by his wife, the evolution of whose views kept step with his own. By virtue of their social inheritance, both of them had access to circles sometimes described as "exclusive." They moved in these circles with the same ease as they moved in any other circle. Absolutely free of the boundaries imposed by class-consciousness, there was no snobbishness in them to inhibit friendships made in any walk of life; similarly, they had none of the inverted snobbery which would have kept them away from the haute monde of their own "class." The moment Mosley's letter to the Prime Minister was published, the social guillotine fell. Henceforward, their political convictions made them social outcasts. Because Lady Cynthia's husband had joined the Labour Party, she was no longer welcomed in many places where previously she had been received with pleasure and delight. Mosley himself was expelled, with solemn ritual, from the 1900 Club - a bland ignoring of the fact that, many months earlier, he happened of his own accord to have resigned from that elite body! Neither Mosley nor his wife were to be intimidated by any kind of persecution, let alone by social ostracism, and although they were doubtless disappointed at the superficial values and lack of proportion shown by their former friends, they dismissed these incidents with a shrug of the shoulders, and concentrated on the job in hand, which was to help the Labour Party in its struggle to secure a fair deal for the masses of the people.

In explaining to the public the reasons for his new allegiance, Mosley said many things which throw light on his approach to public affairs. Politics as a means for the marshalling and counter-marshalling of mere expedients had always appalled him, and to his new colleagues he now ascribed his own fervid desire for an entirely new concept of government. Granting an interview to the Press in April 1924, he described the mentality of the old parties as the "mind of reaction confronting with gloomy and inert pessimism the pain and squalor that it believes to be inherent in human nature, and dismissing with derisive laugh the idealistic vision of a more human and splendid future." He told the reporters that, in his view, the spirit of service must be substituted for that of competition. "It seems to me," he said, "an inevitable change to which all progressive movements tend. This new spirit of service is stronger in the Labour Party than in any other. It is not so much a merely political spirit as a religious one." In that last sentence lies the whole secret of Mosley's driving force. While all politicians have been following personal and party advantages, Mosley has looked upon the just and proper ordering of public life as a religious duty as sacred as any obligation which humanity has been called upon to perform. If the inherent nobility of man is not to be developed and enshrined in the corporate structure of his life, asks Mosley in effect, where else may it flourish without that structure standing in derisive mockery of its pretensions? Thus does he cut through the murky bourgeois concepts which set much store on religious appearances while encouraging political and economic practices which are a denial of every true religious impulse.

6 - Society Is Shocked

It is this sense of religious purpose, together with a profound faith in his fellow-men that survives every disappointment, which has inspired Mosley throughout his career and which today makes certain his victory. Time after time he has expressed this faith in fine and moving language, and never more finely than in the days of vicissitude following his adherence to Labour. In one article of this period he wrote: "Two distinct and conflicting mentalities are preparing to battle for the mastery of the world, one of which is the mind of progress inspired to great exertions by the agonies which surround it, infused by the grandeur of belief in the great destiny of men, and determined to win through at all costs to a nobler order of the world." A few months earlier, debating the fundamentals of human nature with the Duke of Northumberland, he brought his speech to this magnificent close: "The Duke has painted man as a hunted being doomed to destruction by his own heredity, and a fugitive panic-stricken, stumbling through the haunted twilight to extermination. I ask you, on the other hand, to see man with all his faults as the immortal child of Evolution, turning his back upon his ape-like origins, guided surely by the fostering hand of his Creator - mankind turning its anguished face towards a new and happier order, illuminated by the radiance of an ultimate beauty and an ineffable peace."

How little most of his contemporaries allowed themselves to understand Mosley's idealism may be gauged by the tone of the Press criticisms when he decided to fight for it in the ranks of the Labour Party. There was *The Evening Standard's* description of him as a political renegade and of his career as a political rake's progress, a description which the whole Press of the big interests echoed in unison. It was left to a Staffordshire paper, however, to reflect most faithfully the impact which his new political allegiance made on the old-world mind. This was its exquisite summing-up of the position. "We scarcely know which of Mr. Oswald Mosley's many ancestors would have been the more scandalised by his association however temporary in character, with the Labour Party, but probably none of them would have

55

taken it more to heart than his illustrious great-grandfather, Sir Tonman Mosley, who played Grand Seigneur to perfection and commanded the respect of all who knew him." Such a gem defies comment, but one must remark that this pained little journal was not alone in wishing that Oswald Mosley would abandon the political fight so as to play the Grand Seigneur in his native Staffordshire. At the present time, indeed, its Editor would be surprised at the number and influence of his associates.

The Liberal Press, previously so full of flattery while angling for a powerful recruit, turned round in characteristic fashion and snarled at him, leading the pack in violent denunciation. A notable - if one is now inclined to think comic - exception was the *Manchester Guardian*, which congratulated Mr. MacDonald "on the fine young recruit he has secured in the person of Mr. Oswald Mosley." Amidst all the welter of abuse one other journal had the grace to stand up for the truth, referring to Mosley's "great courage, considerable gifts of speech, unquestioned sincerity, and fine and generous spirit."

Mosley's spirit was not only fine and generous - in one sense, not greatly to be deplored, it was too generous. This it was which betrayed him into opinions which later he found untenable. Like all the other Labour members, for instance, he believed at that time in the democratic system. All that was wrong with it, in his view, was that it had got into the wrong hands; when the right men came along it could be made to function in the right way - that was, for the benefit of the people as a whole. He believed that the Labour Party was destined to furnish the right men. Incorruptible himself, he did not foresee that the system would have power to encompass the corruption - spiritually, at least - of the Labour leaders. In 1924 he had no glimmering of the bitter betrayal of the nation which they were to achieve in 1929. It was not until later that he came to realise that the rottenness of parliamentary democracy defied the wit of man to make it work as anything other than an instrument at the service of the most powerful minorities. These minorities under capitalism are finance and the great forces of industrial ownership: under Socialism they would be finance (unless world-socialism destroyed the international financiers, a charming dream) and the most powerful trade unions trampling under-foot all other trade unions or national interests in their scramble to serve their own ends. Ascribing to the Labour and Trade Union leaders a sincerity equal to his own, it followed that much of Mosley's idealism did not square with the facts which he himself was the first man in Britain to discover and proclaim. It followed, too, that believing a reformed democracy to be possible in this country, he did not exclude a similar possibility for India. So it was in the world of international politics. Mosley was not alone in wishing the League of Nations well and working for its success, believing that its defects would be corrected with the accession of better men to power. Every man and woman of decent impulse worked and hoped for precisely these ideals.

The difference between Mosley and most of his contemporaries, however, is that whereas he abandons every concept which he finds unworkable, they carry on extolling its praises the further it leads them to perdition. Nothing reveals the man's integrity more clearly. Large masses of people are always to be found who cling to ideas long after realism has exposed those ideas as valueless, but rather than incur the displeasure of the electorate, democratic politicians flatter it by repeating its favourite catchwords ever more loudly the higher the rising tide of facts that threatens to engulf the people. Mosley refuses to do that. His consistency is unswerving obedience to principle, not to formula. The reader might ask himself which is the grander consistency, the larger honesty - that which clings to a discredited method rather than face a charge of inconsistency, or that which, in pursuance of an ideal, scraps every method that will not serve its purposes and which never hesitates to seek a better way, a firmer, more practical approach? It is not to be supposed that Mosley is the only man in contemporary politics who has become convinced that parliamentary democracy is a fraud, and that by its very structure it can never be anything else. Yet what other man has had the courage to tell the British people that this ideal of theirs is a false ideal which they must ruthlessly scrap if progress is ever to be made and the present headlong decline of the nation ever to be arrested? Not one, and for the reason so vividly illustrated by Mosley's own career - that to tell unwelcome truths is never at first a popular proceeding, and that to tell the truth about the present economic and political system is to bring crashing down upon one the whole weight of the modern racket, Capitalist and Socialist alike. Although Mosley emerges from this ordeal tempered by its fires, the politicians look in askance and prefer to leave the people in a Fool's Paradise rather than incur the hatred of those whose interest it is to keep them there. That is why we find them concealing the breakdown of democracy with parrot-cries about "our sacred democratic liberties" and other farcical catchwords too familiar to be named. This is no apologia for Mosley's changes of view as to the methods whereby his aims may best be obtained. What is set down here is written not in apology but in admiration and pride. The grandest honesty is that which does not traffic with expediency nor hesitate to risk the reproach of "turn-coat" when it recognises that what was once considered a royal road has proved a slippery slope to ruin, necessitating an entirely new approach. That honesty Mosley possesses to the nth degree. They say, his enemies, that his trial of the democratic method invalidates his rejection of it. Is not the exact opposite more likely to be the truth, that the eager and enthusiastic support he gave to it, the full energy of some of the best years of his life which he lavished upon it, confirms and fortifies the reasons which he now advances for its abandonment?

As yet, however, Mosley's faith in the Labour movement and in the amenability to reform of the democratic method was still intact, and strong in that faith, he began his devoted service to its cause. Soon afterwards the power of financial capitalism to make or unmake governments was manifested in a successful effort to drive the Labour Party from office and to keep it from office for another five years by one of the most disgraceful election "ramps" in the history of British politics - the notorious swindle known as the "Zinovieff Letter" scare.

7 - *Honours To Zinovieff*

Mosley's resounding successes on the Labour platform - he spoke for them all over the country - led to his being invited to contest over eighty seats, many in Labour strongholds where his return would have been certain. Instead of seeking a safe seat he decided to look for a hard fight against a man of some importance among his political foes. This man he found in the Ladywood Division of Birmingham. If at any period in his career Mosley had been asked which individual stood out in his mind as the most typical representative of the liaison between Westminster and the City of London he would probably have said "Neville Chamberlain." When in 1924 the opportunity came to tilt an electoral lance against Chamberlain, therefore, it is not surprising that he should have jumped at it. He reluctantly said goodbye to his faithful Harrow, where many members of his local organisation had followed him *en bloc* into the Labour ranks, and set out for "Brum."

The piece of legislation identified with Chamberlain which Mosley found most lamentable was his infamous Rent Act, which placed the large class of tenants almost entirely at the mercy of the relatively small class of landlords. It enabled the landlord, if he could get rid of his tenant, to charge what rent he liked to the next tenant, and use was made of this clause in a large number of instances to impose extortionate rents. Moreover, to help the landlord get rid of his tenant, the Act was accompanied by a Bill which gave him eight new ways of eviction. Mosley began the attack in his usual uncompromising fashion:- "I assert that Mr. Neville Chamberlain's Rent Act is the most monstrous piece of class legislation that ever disgraced the Statute Book of Great Britain. If Mr. Chamberlain resents my words, if he considers my description unfair, then I challenge him to meet me in a public debate upon the subject of the Rent Act - or for that matter upon any other subject."

Neville Chamberlain's reply was not the last word in wisdom. "Mr. Mosley," he said, "comes out with a challenge to debate the Rent Act with him in public. That is a very old trick, which is always played by people who think they can get a little more limelight at the heels of others who have made more noise in the world than themselves." Only Chamberlain's fanatical Tory hatred of Mosley could have betrayed him into so foolish an assault against such a deadly debater. Placing an unerring finger on Neville's signal failures in the Ministry of National Service, in Housing and at the Exchequer, Mosley replied: "I am afraid that Mr. Neville Chamberlain is confusing himself with his father. For what noise has Mr. Chamberlain made in the world? Hoisted by his father's name into great positions, the only noise that he himself made was the noise of the crash when he failed and fell."

On another occasion Mosley had expressed his view about Chamberlain's affinity with modern capitalism by describing him as a "political hireling of the landlord class." Chamberlain professed a sense of personal outrage, and was at great pains to vindicate a personal honour that had not, in fact, been assailed. He had not, he declared, with injured innocence, been "paid" by any class to represent its interests, and Mr. Mosley, "if a gentleman," was required to apologise. Mosley plunged through this snuffling humbug by reiterating the charge and asserting: "I do not suggest that he is paid by the landlords, but I do state most emphatically that his political position, and that of his party, depends entirely upon the support of the landlord class and the great vested interests, and any Conservative has to toe the line to the landlords and the vested interests, who run the Party." Since there is packed into this one sentence the whole gravamen of the charge which the modern movement brings against all the existing political parties, Chamberlain's reply possesses an interest far beyond what appears on the surface. "Mr. Mosley has not withdrawn or apologised," he said. "He has merely tried to wriggle out of it by saying that he did not mean what he said." That was all!

Mosley's speeches were tremendous. At the Birmingham Town Hall he was accorded something resembling a Roman triumph. A member of the audience has left on record the following impression of the occasion: "The Town Hall was packed from floor to ceiling, and over 1,000 turned away. Oswald Mosley spoke for one hour and twenty minutes, and had an ovation when he sat down; cheering continued till finally stopped by the chairman, who said 'In all sincerity it is the greatest speech ever delivered from this platform.' Old men went up to him after, saying: 'Back to Joey, back to the great tradition'! One old man said, 'I have heard Bright, Joseph Chamberlain, Lloyd George, and all the giants of the past at the summit of their powers, but never anything like this meeting. The only thing comparable with this was Joe at the very height and vigour of his manhood.' A Tory present said, 'Nothing like it save Joe's seventieth birthday meeting in the Bingley Hall.'"

Mosley threw the whole of his vigour into the campaign, as did Lady Cynthia, who had always given him magnificent help at Harrow, and who now tirelessly canvassed the poorer quarters of Ladywood. Loyal help was forthcoming from the Labour supporters, and right up to the eve of the poll victory was certain. Then came the Zinovieff letter.

Ever since the revolution in Russia Communist propaganda has been pouring into this country with the object of strengthening the subversive movement here and sowing the seeds of sedition among the armed forces of the Crown. Most of it was intercepted and destroyed by the British authorities. Typical of this propaganda was a document (which may or may not have been a forgery) said to bear the signature of the Communist functionary Zinovieff, and containing elaborate, if rather infantile, instructions for the formation of "propaganda cells" in all units of the troops, in factories working on munitions, and at military store depots, together with suggestions for forming a group, "the future directors of the British Red Army," which was to secure the co-operation of the more talented of the military specialists who had for one reason or another left the Service. Mr Ramsay MacDonald and his Labour colleagues had as much to do with this document as the man in the moon, and rather less, if the latter be indeed the patron saint of lunacy. Yet the newspapers throughout the length of the country published the letter beneath flaming "scare" headlines, depicting the British Empire as being in peril of imminent destruction, cunningly linking the British Labour Party with the silly business and calling upon the electorate to vote for the Conservative Party to protect their country and their homes. Publication was timed for the day before the election, so that it was impossible for the Labour Party to expose the bluff and disassociate themselves from its implications. The result was a helter-skelter stampede into the Conservative camp, and Labour suffered a catastrophic defeat.

Thus it is possible for a supposedly adult nation to be scared out of its wits by newspaper lies. Thus does Government by the people for the people prove itself one of the most monstrous pieces of humbug ever invented by the bourgeois mind. Thus do "our glorious democratic liberties" boil down to the license of money-power to keep the country fit for swindling profiteers, scheming politicians, and lying Press Lords to inhabit. Had MacDonald listened to Mosley, incidentally, he would have been spared this particular ramp. Mosley urged him to dissolve the previous summer by inviting defeat on some legislative measure of first-class social importance, and thus go to the country on a vital issue, but MacDonald chose - in what became his own notorious fashion - to cling to his office until the last possible moment, irrespective of the indignity and fatuousness which an untenable position entails.

Not least among the absurdities of the stampede was that it lost the Ladywood seat for a great Englishman and patriot and sent back to Parliament Mr. Neville Chamberlain as a modern, drab St. George to offer heroic battle to a dragon that existed nowhere outside the scare headlines of a thoroughly disreputable Press.

7 - Honours To Zinovieff

An idea of the tremendous fight put up by Mosley may be gathered from the tiny and even dubious margin of his defeat, despite the overwhelming weight of the Zinovieff scare, which the Birmingham papers played up no less successfully than their London contemporaries. I say "dubious" because to this day it is not at all clear that he was in fact defeated. The final figures were officially announced as being:-

Chamberlain   13,374
Mosley   13,297

This showed a margin of seventy-seven votes in Chamberlain's favour, but this figure was only reached after many counts. The original count showed a majority of seven for Chamberlain; the next a majority of two for Mosley. The final count, conducted amongst great excitement, was not concluded until 4.20a.m, when the wretched members of the counting staff were completely exhausted. The Labour supporters present in the gallery, already enraged by the Zinovieff ramp, were lashed into fury by this most unsatisfactory conclusion to the campaign, and the usual vote of thanks to the officials were drowned in the ensuing hubbub. Mosley seriously considered the advisability of demanding a fresh count, and was only deterred by the thought of the enormous expense in which it would have involved the Labour Party.

One amusing - if scarcely edifying - result of the election was that although the Chamberlains had held the seat for sixty years Neville, disliking so close a shave, seized the first opportunity to abandon it in favour of a strong Conservative constituency. "Safety First" is ever the motto of Democracy's heroes.

The time and energy which Mosley would have devoted to the cause in the House were not lost to the Labour movement. Mosley and his wife redoubled their efforts, and in 1935 Cynthia Mosley allowed herself to be nominated as prospective Labour candidate for Stoke-on-Trent, an association which is still remembered with happiness and pride by the people of the Potteries. In this year, too, they went to India to study its political problems, meeting Indians of every class and creed and thoroughly investigating the views of resident Europeans, both official and unofficial. The conclusions which Mosley then reached are no less interesting because he has since found it necessary to amend them in the light of his experience of the workings of the democratic system in Britain. He objected - as today he would object still more strenuously - to the Round Table conference method of meetings between British and Indian politicians, because that method simply resulted in the disunited Indians uniting to oppose any British proposal, which to them, was always suspect. Therefore he advocated that the Indians should draw up their own proposals before Britain was asked to arrive at a decision.

His object was twofold. First, the Indian representatives, rent by internal differences, would almost certainly fail to agree on any policy, and in that event the maintenance of a strong British government would be justified before the world. Second, if they did succeed in agreeing on any policy, it would almost certainly be acceptable to Britain, because the various Indian factions were so afraid of each other, and hated each other so much, that they could never unite on any policy which left them at the mercy of each other, with the result that any policy on which they agreed would be founded on the maintenance of British authority. His object was thus to stop the game of the Indians uniting for no better purpose than to oppose every British suggestion, and to expose their fundamental disunity, which has since been clearly demonstrated, but which he discerned in advance of most people in this country. Had Mosley's proposals been adopted there would have been less talk, less violence, less disintegration than there has been during the last ten years. At the same time it is true enough that Mosley did believe that the ultimate solution of India's problems would probably be found in some system of parliamentary democracy. He does not hesitate to admit it, any more than he now hesitates to withdraw from a position found to be insupportable. His work in this country, where there are no fundamental cleavages of race and creed, has convinced him that it is impossible for the community interest of the British people to secure representation under a system designed for their economic exploitation, and on that account he now holds it to be an iniquitous thing to hand over to the Indian people the means for their own oppression at the hands of Babu political puppets serving the interests of the mill owners, who are themselves the dupes and agents of international finance. Mosley sees that the best and happiest future for India lies in the encouragement of its agriculture, not in allowing the sub-continent to become a vast semi-urban slum where coolie labourers would be sweated to their own hurt and the final ruin of Lancashire. To secure that future authoritarianism is no less necessary than it is to secure for the British people a future in which economically they can call their souls their own.

On returning home Mosley and Lady Cynthia continued their work for the Labour movement with unabated zeal. At this time Mosley was making a deep study of the financial system, having realised that in its extraordinary power of leverage in the hands of unscrupulous manipulators lay the greater part of the threat to civilisation. The steady evolution of his mind towards forms of corporate control is revealed in proposals made during this period, although it is natural that these proposals were no more than experimental in relation to his present policy. What he wished the Labour Party to do immediately on accession to power was to pass through Parliament a measure for the socialisation of banking, and by this means to establish a minimum wage throughout industry. "Extend credit," he said, "put more money into the hands of the people to buy, and consequently create a demand for the manufacture of goods" - a development of those early ideas of a great home market expounded in the Harrow days, and a link with his present ideas. He defended his proposals against the cry of "inflation" which rose from the camp of "orthodox" finance, insisting that inflation could not rise if the supply of goods were commensurately increased. He granted that under *laissez-faire* conditions inflation would certainly arise in an orgy of luxury spending and speculation, but affirmed that the Labour Party would go straight to the necessitous areas of poverty to arrange for the distribution of the new credits. As the banks issued producers' credits to produce for non-existent markets, Labour would issue consumers' credits wherever purchasing power was low, and thereby create a large demand for the necessities of life. Proper wages would be regarded as the first charge on industry. Mosley asked his colleagues to realise the enormous possibilities of this socialisation of the banks. He pointed out that banking was the key position of capitalism. Let them capture it and the whole system would be at their mercy. "Every capitalist must come to you, and you can dictate the conditions under which he will carry on. We must be able to choose between one condition and another. Here are enormous possibilities of dominating the whole field of capitalism and by one bold stroke to capture its inmost fortress."

These passages show that while his colleagues were still cluttering up their minds with cumbrous plans for the regimentation of industry under public ownership, Mosley conceived a bold, swift stroke for gaining the mastery of the whole situation which made those plans redundant. In the course of time he was to simplify this project through the discovery that the full powers of control inherent in the corporate system dispensed even with the need for socialising the banks, since they would find themselves relentlessly guided by that system to canalise credit along socially useful channels with the certainty of jail for those of their directors who might refuse. In other words, Mosley has come to see that most genuine Socialist thought is preoccupied with arranging to carry the horse of the nation's economic life, whereas all that is required is to lead that horse in whatever direction an authoritarian government acting for the people wishes it to go. Another factor which was then being forced upon Mosley's attention was the impossibility of a high-wage system side by side with an open-door fiscal policy. Confronted with this choice, there is no politician who dares to prefer the high-wage system to the open-door, or at any rate to the nearly open door. Mosley did dare, greatly to the alarm of the capitalist world. He began to advocate the exclusion of sweated goods.

While defending his financial proposals against the charge of "inflation" Mosley vigorously counter-attacked on the ground of "deflation" so dear to the banking interests and the rentier class and so wantonly followed by British Governments for many weary years. He exposed "deflation" for the sordid ramp it was - a bankers' ramp and a ramp on behalf of the owners of fixed-interest bearing bonds, whose income was doubled while industry was starved both for credit and for a market still desperately in need of credit. He pointed out the evils of a system in which industry was obliged to buy its raw materials at one price-level and sell its products in the ebb of falling prices, resulting sometimes in bankruptcy and always in increased unemployment. He had a glimpse of the confusion and tragedy that lay ahead in the near future. He saw Churchill subscribing to the general madness by the reintroduction of the Gold Standard. Almost alone of his contemporaries he laid his hand upon the real dangers and evils of the time, and was consequently marked down by the powers of Press and Purse. The famous Smethwick by-election in 1926 was to provide them with an opportunity of showing what they could do when they tried. That was also the year when a greedy, lunatic capitalism, bewildered by the chaos of world competition and its own anarchy at home, decided to solve the problem of an inadequate purchasing power by wage-cuts which would make it more inadequate still, thereby plunging the country into the perils of the General Strike.

8 - The Battle Of Smethwick

The fear which the labour advent to office awakened in the guardians of the old order had to some extent been stilled by its moderately good behaviour in general, and by the exemplary behaviour of Mr. Snowden at the Exchequer, where nothing was done to impair the excellent relationship normally existing between Westminster and the City. Labour had not achieved power, in the sense of a clear majority, and that factor was not neglected in computing the possibilities of the future, but even so the old world was not greatly perturbed. It has a sure instinct in these matters, and having observed the first Labour Ministry at work it no longer saw reason to entertain thoughts of panic about the future of its bank balances and financial power as a whole, although it naturally preferred its Baldwins and Churchills to the new men who had not yet been trained to its purposes. The Zinovieff bomb having been exploded with shattering effect, there was for some time a diminution in the violence of its anti-Socialist tirades, a diminution which represented the amiable attitude of men who feel tolerantly towards the foes whose measure they have taped. The much dreaded Labour Party - what was it after all, they whispered, but another Liberal Party? Its policy of the Inevitability of Gradualness was admirable; properly managed, that policy would lead to the inevitability of the Labour Party becoming part and parcel of their own capitalist racket.

So long as Labour was a good, laborious cart-horse plodding its way to some distant millennium, then all in their view was assuredly well. But no sooner had they settled down in this complacent attitude than a young man appeared before their horrified gaze riding the beast with such dynamic energy that it showed every sign of transforming itself into a veritable war-horse, offering instant battle for the key position of their whole system. That was more than their nerves could stand, especially since they had had previous experience of this young man and knew something of his courage and skill. They were driven back into the vortices of their fear and lashed out in a frenzy of self-protection. Processes for the mass production of abuse and derision were again invoked. The bankers, anxious as ever to defend the system which gave them their power and wealth, set their experts to work denouncing Mosley's new banking proposals and depicting their advocate as a crank of whom no notice should be taken. Press and Pulpit and Platform for the next year were vigorously engaged in taking a great deal of notice of him, however, so that in the end his name was more than ever a household word. The lordly Times rushed in to sing the praises of "Britain's incomparable banking system." Its correspondence columns were filled for weeks with letters suggesting that the poverty amidst plenty entailed in that "incomparable system" was economically insuperable and, indeed, no little matter for self-congratulation. "Sound" financiers enjoyed an orgy of boosting the virtues of "sound" finance, while millions were unemployed and millions more desperately poor because of the failure of finance to meet their needs. The provincial newspapers vied with London in dismissing Mosley with contempt and calling upon Britons to rejoice in a system which kept them poor.

Mosley was in no way disconcerted. He carried his crusade to every part of the country. The impact of his vigorous young mind galvanised the Labour Party into new life. Article and letters shot from his pen in a constant blaze of attack. They were reinforced by an extremely able pamphlet, "Revolution by Reason," in which his views were amplified and all the difficulties in the path of his monetary proposals boldly set down and answered. The Press pounced upon the pamphlet to tear it to pieces and nullify its effect. The result was that its effect was ten times more devastating than if they had given it a more approving glance. Mosley was now famous. Wherever he appeared he was greeted with a thunderous welcome, and the custodians of the old order were more than ever determined that he should be destroyed.

8 - The Battle Of Smethwick

The line they took was to try to damage him in the eyes of the masses whom he championed by a concerted enfilade of sneers about his independent means and Lady Cynthia's title. Pictures were dug out of the archives showing both of them on holiday in Italy and the South of France. It was represented as a lamentable piece of humbug that people professing to be Socialists should have gone on holiday to pleasant places abroad. More than that, it was said to be scandalous for moneyed people to pretend to be Socialists. So steeped in mercenary liberalism was the prevailing atmosphere that Mosley's enemies could think of no better way of hounding him out of public life than by dwelling upon what they declared to be the impossibility of any man or woman, possessing that accident of a wealthy inheritance, genuinely believing in a new and finer dispensation or the better and more equitable distribution of the world's wealth.

According to their philosophy a man's heart and soul could not move a single inch beyond the confines of his pocket: greed was the universal law of life - or so they seemed to assume in their disgraceful attack on Mosley and his wife. If these two were sincere - so ran the argument - then they would give up all their money. It was a quaint argument. How two people were to assist in the work of raising the masses from a needless beggary by reducing themselves to a needless beggary the critics made no attempt to explain, any more than they attempted to explain away the fact that by surrendering their private means under the existing system the Mosleys would merely have put back into the pockets of the financiers further ammunition for their own destruction as the champions of the people. Cynthia Mosley answered her yelping critics with cutting simplicity when she declared: "No doubt it is sound Conservative doctrine that those who are not themselves in miserable conditions should do nothing to help those who are living in miserable conditions. This, however, is not a Socialist doctrine. As a Socialist I put myself and any resources the freaks of this system gave me at the disposal of the workers in the great struggle to change this evil system into a more human system." But the hounds of the Press and party politics were amenable neither to the promptings of honesty nor of logic. They continued to depict the Mosleys as hypocrites whom the working classes in their own interests should reject. Their attack rose in a crescendo of misrepresentation and abuse. That Lady Cynthia dressed herself decently instead of appearing in rags, that she possessed jewels as part of her family heirlooms, that she retained her title - these things were all used as evidence of her own insincerity and that of her husband. Particularly nauseating were the chatterbox journals of Britain's decadent "Society," with their references to whatever gown she happened to be wearing as "contrasting so oddly, my dears, with her very advanced Socialist ideas - and then there is that title!" The Press even trumped up a story that Lady Cynthia had told her audiences to call her "plain Mrs. Mosley" - an absolute lie. That the argument about the title carried weight with people enslaved to bourgeois values is clear enough from the almost inevitable questions at meetings. The attitude of Lady Cynthia, like the attitude of Mosley towards his later title, was too simple for many people to understand. Title simply did not count. "Sir" and "Lady" were no more significant than "Mr." or "Mrs.," and therefore no more necessary to renounce. Renunciation would have given them an importance they did not possess: it would have been an inverted snobbery. It might have "paid" Mosley to refuse his title and Lady Cynthia to lay hers aside, but neither was prepared to allow mere appearances to be exalted when the reality was independent of such trifles.

The Press, conscious of its triumphant part in the defeat of the Labour Party in 1924, did not doubt its ability to defeat the Mosleys along the lines indicated. Its opportunity to try conclusions came towards the end of 1926, when a by-election occurred at Smethwick owing to the resignation of the sitting Labour member, and Mosley was nominated by the local association to contest the seat in the Labour interest. There was a small preliminary hitch owing to the nomination being made without any reference to the National Executive, an infringement of one of the rules. The matter was speedily and amicably settled, but this did not prevent the Press hurling itself upon the incident to distort it out of recognisable shape and size. The National Executive, it screamed did not want Mosley to stand. He was too intimately connected with the I.L.P. His currency proposals were not acceptable to Snowden. Snowden did not want him to have the chance of expounding his pet theory on the floor of the House. The local Labour Party was prevailing on Mr. Davison (the retiring member) to withdraw his resignation. The Labour movement was split from top to bottom. And so it went on, the "yes-men" of the Press searching in their silly heads for fresh lies to tell.

In this they were eminently successful, showing inexhaustible resource. The might of the British Press was summoned for no other purpose than to calumniate Mosley. He and his wife were represented one day as Moscow agents; the next day as careerists vainly endeavouring to make the best of both worlds; the next day as shuffling parasites against whom the workers of Smethwick were rising in thousands to drive out of the constituency. Holidays at Biarritz, at Venice, were again dragged into the fray. So were the jibes about dresses and jewels and titles and wealth. Cynthia Mosley was even described as visiting the poorer quarters of Smethwick to tell the women that all they had to do to get "beautiful furs like hers" was to vote for her husband at this election. Then came the beastliest thing in a campaign of indescribable beastliness. Beaverbrook's *Daily Express* induced Mosley's father to take a hand in vilifying his own son. A special interview was arranged, in which Sir Oswald Mosley gave full expression to the bitterness which still rankled from his son's early boyhood. I think it wise to publish the extraordinary statements that he made exactly as they appear in the columns of the *Express*:-

"I could never understand the line my son has taken. He was born with a gold spoon in his mouth - it cost £100 in doctor's fees to bring him into the world. He lived on the fat of the land and never did a day's labour in his life. He had the best education to bring him up, and money spent on him galore! He has a big income from his own family and on the other side. If he and his wife want to go in for Labour, why don't they do a bit of work themselves, or why doesn't Lady Cynthia sell her pearls for the good of the Smethwick poor? And why doesn't she drop her title if she doesn't like it? I understand it is only a courtesy title. I could not drop mine if I wanted to drop it. My son tells the tale that he does this and that, but he lives in the height of luxury. If the working class, for whom I have always stuck up, are going to be taken in by such nonsense - I am sorry for them. How does my son know anything about them?"

Mosley, asked by the *Daily Herald* to comment on this, exercised the severest restraint. "I was removed from the care of my father when I was five years of age by an order of a court of law," he said. "I was placed in the care of my mother, who was legally separated from him. Since that date my father knows nothing of my life and has very seldom seen me. So far as I am aware, he contributed nothing to my education or upbringing, except in the form of alimony which he was compelled to contribute in a court of law."

He might have said a good deal more than this. His years in France, for example, were not altogether without "a day's labour." Neither were the eight strenuous years of his political life, in which he had often worked fourteen hours a day, and at one period without having an evening to himself for three months. He might also have pointed out that, while he did not chose to live in a hovel, there were no excesses that any man in honesty could impute to him. He might justly have said these things because everybody who knows Mosley knows that he is a splendid and tireless worker, and that there has always been a clear-cut simplicity in his personal life and habits. He preferred, however, to reply to his father without a single word of self-defence, and even the one or two sentences he did speak were kept out of the majority of newspapers which published the attack.

8 - The Battle Of Smethwick

It is not the custom of our "free" Press to deal honestly with its opponents, and certainly not when its opponent happens to possess the strength and challenge of a Mosley. The papers redoubled their efforts as the election proceeded. They never mentioned Lady Cynthia without the epithet, "Furs and Fables, a reference to their own lie about what she was supposed to have told the women of Smethwick. Each day they sprang a new lie about Mosley. He had negotiated for the purchase of a farmhouse. This was presented to the nation as "buying a huge mansion." They sent men snooping round the hotel where he had stayed to inquire how much he paid and whether he drank champagne. They said on one page that he drove round the constituency in a luxurious motor-car. On another page, so far forgetting themselves, they declared that, rather than face electors in his own car, he had chosen to hire an old, rickety contraption wherewith to camouflage his wealth. He was described as "pale" and "trembling" in face of questions about that wealth. His questioners "tied him in knots" about his policy. Nobody could have cut a sorrier figure, to judge by their account of his meetings.

Amidst this welter of absurdities and lies Mosley kept remarkably calm, hitting out from time to time with telling effect, but concentrating mainly upon great problems of national reconstruction, and putting forward views about banking which his opponents could only answer with personal abuse and irrelevancies about his wife's dresses and his own clothes. "I was not born with a gold spoon in my mouth," jeered his principal opponent, a Mr. Pike, endeavouring to make capital out of the *Express* interview. Stanley Baldwin, Prime Minister, played a worthy part by suggesting that Mosley could be treated with contempt. All this was a poor answer to Mosley's arguments for a high-wage economy control of the banks, electricity extension, and mobilisation of the national resources of land, coal, power, and transport in one comprehensive and practical plan which could change the face and fortunes of the country. Neither did it dispose of Mosley's indictment of the Government's deflationary policy, which had brought the country to the verge of chaos in the inevitable culmination of discontent in the General Strike. All these things the Press dismissed as "Mosley's Lies," a quaint charge to emanate from this source.

Readers of newspapers in other parts of the country may have been misled about Mosley, his career, his ideals, and his electoral chances, by this infamous newspaper campaign against a man feared and hated by the great vested interests of the land, and marked down by them for political extinction. Englishmen, taking their notion of life from the distorting mirrors of the Press, are sometimes betrayed into grievous injustice and error. But where they have sufficient personal contact to awaken their intuitive faculties, they rarely allow themselves to be led astray. Thus while Lloyd George was perpetuating German enmity against Britain by his reparations policy, British troops on the Rhine were establishing an enduring reputation for British honour and decency and sportsmanship in the hearts of the German people.

Nearly twenty years later, when the Jews were endeavouring to create an ugly riot over the visit of the German football team, the great-hearted British public responded by calling out encouragingly to the bland German captain: "Come on, Snowball!" So it was in Smethwick. Whatever the effect of the Press calumnies elsewhere, the Smethwick people reacted to it with a sense of outrage such as the Press lords could scarcely have foreseen - but it was not against Mosley that their anger was directed. Being simple folk, they held responsible for the orgies of lying the reporters actually present at Mosley's meetings, and on one occasion only Mosley's intervention saved these agents of bigger men from being flung out of the hall by an infuriated band of women. "Do not mind these people," he exhorted. "They are, though they do not know it, just wage-slaves of capitalism. Big owners of newspapers are trying to keep me out of Parliament, and these poor men are paid to write stuff they know to be lies." The incident serves to show that, where the British public has the opportunity of judging for itself, the Press can yell till it is black in the face without influencing its judgement, and at Smethwick the people had had this opportunity, with the result that their intuition left them in no doubt about Mosley's burning honesty, which had been so bitterly assailed.

The last move of the Press was to prepare the country for Mosley's crushing defeat. Smethwick workers, they said, had lost all confidence in him. They would not trust him to represent them on any consideration whatever. The results on polling day were:-

Mosley (Lab.)	16,077
Pike (Con.)	9,495
Bayliss (Lib.)	2,600
Majority	6,582

When the figures were announced, he was given a triumphal progress, huge crowds cheering him as his supporters hauled his car through the streets attached to ropes.

Mosley had multiplied his predecessor's majority by five. "A great victory over Pressocracy," he proclaimed to his triumphant supporters. The Press, deeply chagrined, forgetting that they had announced the certainty of defeat, now declared the result to have been inevitable, due to the unpopularity always incurred by Governments, and to any cause under the sun other than Mosley's indomitable courage, skill, determination, and powers of great leadership, or the splendid and unswerving support he had received from Cynthia Mosley, who had suffered the grossest malignment with an equanimity and resolve equal to his own.

Months afterwards, *The Times* and countless other journals were frittering away their time and energy in the publication of a silly controversy as to whether rich men make good Socialists. The final words on the subject, spiritually at least, were those of the *Bristol Times and Mirror*: "It is doubtful how far the working classes generally will take kindly to this pose of the rich as their potential friends. Many of them must rather share the contempt which Mr. Baldwin expressed for wealth posturing as the sympathiser with poverty." There spoke the soul of the twentieth-century civilisation through the lips of the Berry Press.

The vast conspiracy of vested interests had pitted itself against Mosley and failed in all things except the revelation of its infinite capacity for being foul. Mosley went back to Parliament stronger than ever in his determination to bring into being that new order in which such foulness would lack air to breathe.

9 - *Attack On Labour Finance*

The next move against Mosley could have been predicted. His return to Parliament was written down in terms of bathos. His first speech was declared a fiasco. Whatever reputation he had made in years gone by was now irreparably damaged, according to the reports. He had lost his grip, and there was no Labour member however inexperienced, who did not outshine him in debate. His opportunities for advancement within the party no longer existed: his name was never even mentioned by the Labour leaders in surveying the talent available when the next Labour Ministry should come to be formed. His "self-advertisement" (quaint description) at Smethwick had been vanity of vanities. The man no longer counted. He had signed his own political death warrant.

Mosley's speeches and general prestige soon exposed the absurdity of this new campaign. The first thing that he taught his opponents was that he had lost none of his power of making them look ridiculous when they revived their old tactics of subjecting him to a barrage of jeering interruptions. This was very evident during his speech on the Trades Disputes Act. "We live and learn," he declared, whereupon Sir William Lane Mitchell, the Streatham member, uttered a series of derisive "Hear, hear's." Mosley riposted, "We live and learn - with one notable exception. The Hon. Member for Streatham, alas, has never learned to address this assembly. Long have his constituents waited anxiously for the great day, but they have had to be content with these subterranean gurglings which punctuate our discussions." Sir Victor Warrender, commencing a loud discussion whilst Mosley spoke, was informed that his conversation was more interesting than his speeches. The interruptions of other members were described as "strange noises representing the dumb, instinctive yearning to achieve the flights of human speech." By these means he again commanded the necessary silence in which to make himself heard, and to bring to an end a biting attack on "the most contemptible Government of modern times, which is to be congratulated on having won its power by forgery (a reference to the Zinovieff affair), and used that power for the establishment of slavery."

There was between Churchill and Mosley an enmity of long standing, due to Mosley's early attacks on the Coalition, when Churchill would wait for the uproar to subside and then summon up all his resources in an effort to destroy the effect of those criticisms. "He used to charge down on me like a bull," wrote Mosley reminiscently in after years. The debate on the Budget in 1927 led to a renewal of these old encounters. Churchill attempted to explain away his Budget deficiency by declaring that it had been the fault of the coal stoppage. Mosley took up the challenge. His analysis went very much deeper than the Chancellor's, and revealed Churchill himself as the man to blame. The return to the Gold Standard in his first Budget, Mosley declared, meant that the Chancellor made a gift of £1,000,000,000 to the rentier class, besides increasing the price of all exports by about 10 percent, and placing a burden of 1s. 9d. on every ton of exported coal. The price of British coal in terms of sterling had therefore to be reduced, or else more had to be asked for it in terms of foreign currency. Since the latter course shrunk our markets the sterling price had to be reduced, whereupon the coal owners decided upon a reduction of wages, in which they received every support from the Government whose policy had made this step inevitable.

Mosley followed up this attack with an explanation of his own views on currency and credit expansion, which subject he was determined to keep in the forefront of his campaign - a determination which led to some little commotion in the Labour Party. First hints of the commotion arose from the I.L.P. resolution on the Minority Report of the Colwyn Committee, which was to be discussed at the annual conference of the Labour

Party at Blackpool. The Colwyn Committee had been appointed by the Labour Government to "consider and report on the National Debt and on the incidence of existing taxation, with special reference to their effect on trade, industry, employment, and national credit." At that time the capital levy was the declared policy of Labour for dealing with war debt problems, but both reports of the Colwyn Committee decided against the levy because of the effects of deflation, a policy pursued in accordance with the Cunliffe Committee recommendations of 1919, which recommendations had guided not only the Tories, but Snowden as well. The levy would, therefore, have entailed the repayment of most of the bondholders in money worth nearly double that which they had lent. The Minority proposals of the Colwyn Committee offered an alternative in the shape of a graduated surtax averaging two shillings in the pound on unearned incomes above £500 a year. It was estimated that this would bring in £85,000,000 a year, and suggestions were made for securing extra sums to increase the total to £150,000,000 a year. Of this sum the Minority Report proposed that £50,000,000 should be allocated to an increase in the Sinking Fund for the liquidation of the National Debt, and to this Mosley strongly objected. "Half the proceeds of the new taxation," he wrote, "is to be tamely handed back to the bond-holders from whose income it has just been taken. They are to be repaid in pounds worth double those they lent, instead of the full proceeds of the new taxation being devoted to the working class." He pointed out that after the deduction of £25,000,000 for the abolition of food taxes, only £25,000,000 would be left for the great Labour schemes of education, health, housing, pensions, "all our elementary pledges," to say nothing of plans for increasing purchasing power through the development of family allowances, estimated to cost £120,000,000 a year.

Indications of how Mosley's mind was working towards his present policy abound in this controversy. He admitted that repayments to the bond-holders would lead to the release of more money for industry, but argued that existing machinery was already standing idle; that there would be investments in luxury and other futile trades; that money would be invested abroad still further to finance Britain's competitors; that there would be no public control and no appreciable benefits for the masses, whose ability to consume, on the other hand, was directly and indirectly benefited by money spent on great schemes of social services. "The necessity is a vast home market," he insisted, a lesson which throughout the whole of his career he has been trying to drum into the heads of the politicians. "The market is lacking because the workers do not possess the power to buy what industry can produce." Mosley's strong line led to the following I.L.P. resolution for Blackpool:-"This Conference welcomes the proposal contained in the Minority Report of the Colwyn Committee to impose a special surtax on unearned incomes, but is of the opinion that in present circumstances the proceeds of this surtax should be devoted to Family Allowance and other social purposes instead of to the Sinking Fund." Mosley spoke very forcibly in support, stressing that rapid debt redemption was not an end in itself, affecting the real wealth of the country, but a book-keeping transfer to one lot of rich men to another lot of rich men. The resolution, put as an amendment , was defeated.

Another resolution of the I.L.P. embodied Mosley's proposals for the socialised control of the Banks. It read: "This Conference is of the opinion that the winning of a living wage for workers and the prevention of unemployment is largely dependent on an early change in the banking policy of the country. It condemns the policy of deflation pursued since the war by the Treasury and the Bank of England in the interests of the owning and banking classes, and, regarding as profoundly significant the admission of leading bankers that present financial policy is responsible for the present trade depression, demands that an immediate enquiry be held into the operation of the Bank Act, the revision of which it considers to be an important preliminary to the effective nationalisation of the banking system. It further instructs the Executive Committee to prepare a detailed scheme for presentation to the next Annual Conference, defining the measures for the transfer of the banking system from private to public control."

Arguing in support of this resolution, Mosley went to the heart of the Labour Party's weakness - the orthodox finance of Philip Snowden. "The Labour Chancellor," he wrote, "appeared to be in no way alive to the necessity of a conscious and scientific credit policy ...... His adherence to the Cunliffe Committee recommendations and the Gold Standard objective has throughout prevented the great crimes of Toryism in the creation of unemployment and the reduction of wages been fully brought home to its authors. Labour was not guilty of that crime, but the attitude and commitments of our financial pundits made it difficult to challenge Tory policy effectively and to drive home the lesson to the country ...... It thus seems a little unfortunate that the ex-Labour Chancellor should appear, judging from his article in *The Banker*, to be an ardent supporter of Mr. Montagu Norman. It will be little less than a disaster if in this struggle Labour support is accorded to the reactionary elements in the City. It will certainly be a fantastic negation of the purposes of our Party." Prophetic words, laden with forebodings of the dismal truth of things to come.

Mosley recalled that as long back as 1924 he had challenged Snowden's deflationary policy. "At the time of the appointment of the Colwyn Committee," he wrote, "I asked Mr. Snowden that its terms of reference should include the relation of the debt question to the general policy of deflation recommended by the Cunliffe Committee. This was peremptorily refused, as the Labour Chancellor was 'guided by the report of the Cunliffe Committee.' Yet the Cunliffe policy of deflation has been responsible for nearly doubling the real burden of the national debt ...... Acute deflation with the object of returning to the Gold Standard at pre-war parity has been the policy of this country since the war, in pursuance of the recommendations of the Cunliffe Committee. Deflation, in fact, achieves its object through the creation of unemployment. Credit is restricted and industry slowed up. By this process a surplus of unemployed is created which competes for jobs and thus helps to reduce the wages of those in employment. By the reduction of wages the internal price level is reduced and the foreign exchange forced up until the objective of pre-war parity is reached. The falling price level entails a steady history of industrial losses and bankruptcies. Every manufacturer has to buy his raw material and labour at a higher price level than that in which he sells the finished product. Consequently, they draw in their horns and wait for prices to touch bottom, with the result of trade stagnation ...... Yet in the concluding phase of a policy which, in the opinion not only of Socialists but of most modern economists, has doubled the burden of the national debt, has forced the two greatest industrial struggles of history upon the workers, and has entailed unparalleled wage reductions, Mr. Philip Snowden wrote in the *Financial Times* of December 23, 1926: 'Eighteen months' experience of the operation of the Gold Standard has not brought the disastrous consequences which some people feared....'"

The newspapers were quick to seize upon this conflict of view - which, indeed, was even more a conflict of spirit - and to present it as a fundamental cleavage. The I.L.P. group, they said, was suspicious of the Labour Leaders, believing that they contemplated an alliance with the Liberals, whereas they themselves (the I.L.P.) were looking for support from the Communists. Mosley was represented as holding out strongly against a split. That, at any rate, was true. So long as he saw in the Labour Party even the remotest chance of its pledges being implemented, he set his face against its disintegration into a number of impotent minorities adding to the prevailing chaos of national affairs. He had still to learn to what extent the deadly malaise of political cowardice and opportunism had eaten away the soul of the Labour Party. The path was not made easy for him, even at that time in his endeavour to help forward Party unity without surrendering one jot of his determination for action. After the rejection of his proposals at Blackpool for instance, he was to have opened a discussion on finance in the House, roughly at seven o'clock. At six o'clock the Labour members allowed the House to be "counted out," thereby precluding the possibility of the debate taking place that session.

After this fiasco Mosley's Parliamentary activities were brought to an end for some considerable time, owing to a recurrence of trouble from his old war injuries, which an anonymous Tory writer of the period described in a book as being "politically useful." The suggestion was that Mosley made political capital out of them, whereas the only use they served was as a basis for the Tory lie about Sandhurst. So far from being useful to Mosley they were a cruel handicap, often causing excruciating pain, which was borne with steel. While Cynthia Mosley deputised for her husband during his illness, spending evening after evening on Labour platforms, Mosley occupied the time helping to prepare the pamphlet "Labour and the Nation," and so keen was his desire to infuse life into the Party that he had himself carried to consultations with his colleagues, exactly as he had once had himself carried into the Front Line rather than go to hospital.

Events were now moving towards the General Election, and the fall of the Baldwin Government. The Prime Minister, blind to the anarchy caused by the free play of undisciplined economic forces, admitted his bankruptcy of ideas by informing the farmers of Worcestershire, that he "rejoiced to see industrial problems taken out of the hands of the politicians, who had never been fit to handle them." Mosley swept to the attack. "This view," he declared, "leads many of us to inquire what is the function of a modern government if it has no concern with industrial problems. Every major problem of modern politics is an industrial problem. Unemployment, wages, housing, and industrial conditions - these are the things that matter today. They are all industrial problems, but, according to Mr. Baldwin, the State must not meddle with such matters. All lesser things fade into oblivion before the great spectre of unemployment and the horror of present industrial conditions. Yet Conservatives say to any Government, 'Hands off!' Here is the real and fundamental issue between us."

He followed up his attack with a challenging declaration of faith: "At the forthcoming election we proclaim that a Socialist Government must be a Government of activity and achievement. We believe that unemployment and our other problems can be handled by resolute government. They can never be solved by a creed of indifference and despair. These pleasant, sleepy people are all very well in pleasant, sleepy times, but we live in a dynamic age of great and dynamic events. In such an age we summon all classes to a united effort of the whole nation in the war against poverty." This note of challenge was sounded with great persistence by Mosley, who went so far as to write in a party journal that what he was afraid of was not that a Labour Government might do too much, but that it might do too little. A member of the National Executive, he had already had a tussle with MacDonald, Snowden and Co. over the Election programme. He wanted it short and concise; they wanted it vague and verbose. Even so, he gave them full credit for sharing his own enthusiasm, even if not his own implacable resolve. He was not too easy in his mind about their courage, although he could not foresee quite how disastrously feeble it was to prove.

Mosley held his seat at Smethwick, and Lady Mosley captured Stoke-on-Trent after a campaign which her opponent conducted mainly on the ground of her wealth. The figures were:-

Stoke-on-Trent

Cynthia Mosley	26,548
Col. Ward	18,689
Majority	7,859

Smethwick

Mosley	19,550
Wise (Con.)	12,201
Marshall (Lib.)	3,909
Majority	7,349

The Labour Party was returned to office, once again without

that clear majority which would have destroyed its last craven excuse for "sitting tight" and refusing to carry out a single item of its great programme of social reconstruction.

MacDonald now had the task of choosing his Ministry and recourse should be had to Scanlan's brilliant book "The Decline and Fall of the Labour Party" in order to appreciate the atmosphere in which the selections were made. It was deplorable beyond description. Not even post-war unemployment queues were quite so long as that of the job hunters who lined up outside MacDonald's office, as it were; licking their chops over the rewards which they believed to be their due. It seemed as though every Labour pundit of even the remotest district expected to be called in to assist in the government of the country. Herein may perhaps be found some explanation of the appalling failure of the Labour Party. Despite the selfless devotion of so many of its rank and file, the movement itself was not charged with the spirit of service and sacrifice. Even in theory its economic policy was seen by most in as grossly materialistic a light as the system it was supposed to supplant, while politically its opportunism and divorce from its own ideals were as egregious an example of opportunism as any that has disgraced the public life of Britain.

Although Mosley, as was to be expected, held scornfully aloof from the scramble for jobs, and despite the revolt he was leading against Snowden's financial orthodoxy, his claims could not be denied. His immense prestige in the party, the extraordinary vigour of his mind, his brilliance in debate, his powers of leadership - all these things demanded that he should be given a part to play in the Labour administration, and he was accordingly made Chancellor of the Duchy of Lancaster, and accepted a special brief to act with Thomas, Lansbury, and Tom Johnston in tackling the unemployment problem. It was upon the pledge of the Labour Party to solve this problem that it had been returned to office. A wave of relief and hope was animating the whole of the working classes. The poor and the oppressed were confident that at last the power of vested interests would be subordinated to national welfare, and that the reign of poverty amidst plenty would come speedily to an end.

Nobody could have been more determined that their hope and faith should not be betrayed than Oswald Mosley, youngest Minister to hold so responsible a post for half a century.

10 - Mosley Versus Snowden And Thomas

J.H. Thomas, faced at the outset with mounting unemployment, proceeded to act in characteristic fashion. Mosley's first-class brains, and the life long experience of industrial conditions possessed by his two other colleagues, were altogether ignored. Thomas started upon his mission without even calling them into consultation. He preferred a lone hand, probably because he was jealous of Mosley's superior ability. It was in this spirit that he drew up certain makeshift measures designed to give work; mainly devices for the encouragement of local authorities to put in hand schemes of public utility. Mosley gave him loyal support in the attempt to achieve an initial success. He wound up debate after debate for the Government, defending Thomas with a skill and increasing grip over detail which commanded for him the respect of all disinterested observers, although his enemies still depicted him as a sort of licensed clown floundering in his own stupidity. Particular attention was paid to one incident in which Thomas repaid Mosley's loyalty by letting him down in a bare faced manner. He instructed him to give the House the figure £7,000,000,000 as the cost of a projected railway electrification scheme. "These figures are fantastic," declared Mosley. Thomas assured him that they were accurate, and on this understanding Mosley quoted them in his speech. They were promptly challenged by the Opposition, whereupon Thomas entered the House and indulged in the pantomimics of getting his colleague out of a mess, never revealing the fact that they were his own figures. The papers threw the blame for this fiasco upon Mosley.

In spite of incidents of this sort Mosley never wavered in his support, and in particular he threw enormous energy into urging upon local councils the need to take advantage of the Government's offers. He knew that the schemes in relation to the unemployment problem were little more than a drop of water in relation to the ocean; he knew that many local authorities were turning the Government's grants into ramps for favoured contractors; he knew that there was a hopeless lack of co-ordination in the carrying out of the measures. At the same time he knew that there was an urgent necessity for a start to be made and machinery created whereby the more far-reaching programme of the Labour Party could be carried into effect.

During this period it fell to his lot to interview deputations from local councils all over Britain, who came to see him about a variety of proposals, nearly all complicated and some presenting remarkable difficulty. Many members of these deputations afterwards expressed their amazement at the breadth and depth of Mosley's mind and the way in which it cut through all exterior wrappings to dive into the core of their troubles and divine precisely their needs. There was no longer any doubt in the minds of discerning judges that here was Labour's future Prime Minister.

Mosley got on with the job in hand, making not the slightest attempt to curry favour with colleagues who might have a voice in the bestowal of this high position. His temperament in any event would have inhibited fawning and flattering. John Beckett, a Labour member at that period, and now, in these more difficult and turbulent days, one of Mosley's ablest and most fearless lieutenants, admirably describes the impression made on him by the young Minister: "Mosley had the worst possible temperament for success at Westminster as it exists today," he has written. "He suffered fools badly; he wanted to work - not listen for hours to the wearisome babblings of decrepit Trade Union leaders sent to the House of Commons as a place of pension when all further prospects of work for them in any other capacity had gone. Neither was O.M. a success with the numerous and influential night-club coterie in the smoking-room off the terrace. I have seen other recruits like Sir Stafford Cripps or Dr. Dalton spending hours walking from one simple Labour member to another, slipping their arms over their shoulders and listening with charm to their reminiscences. This explains why, for the first time in the history of the Labour movement, a wealthy man of good family did not remain popular. Outside in the country, until the barrage of the caucus was brought to bear, Mosley was the most popular figure we had. Inside, the caucus had long begun to suspect him of a desire to disturb their comfort and peace."

Even the small preparatory schemes drawn up by Thomas and strenuously pushed by Mosley, set in motion the insensate opposition of the Tories. Churchill led the attack. Then the dictators of Britain decided to raise the Bank Rate. Money was imperatively in demand for national purposes; therefore money was to be withheld. Mosley was bitter. "For every man the Government put in work, the banks can put two men out of work," he declared. But Snowden made no effort to place the banks under control and thus prevent sabotage. Turning to the question of Churchill, Mosley asked contemptuously: "What are we to think of the conduct of Mr. Churchill, who by his policy reduced the country to its present condition, and now can find nothing better to do than to stand amid the ruins of his own creation, mocking and deriding the efforts of his successors to repair the devastation he has wrought? He is like a man who, in a spirit of wanton malice, sets light to a house and then throws stones at the fire brigade." There was obstruction in the House of Lords. Much needed energy had to be side tracked to reach a compromise in this quarter. It was clear to Mosley that nothing could be done to stop the dry rot except with an entirely new drive that would break through the cordons of reaction and impose the strong will of Government upon all the disruptive forces and vested interests which stood athwart its path.

Meanwhile, having launched his little boats upon the ocean of unemployment, Thomas sat down and scratched his head, and that appeared to be the limit of his resources. The world was moving towards the crash of 1931. Unemployment resisted all ordinary methods to deal with it. The millions of men and women who had slaved with unswerving self-sacrifice for the

Portrait of a Leader

Labour Party during many years, who had contributed their hard earned coppers to the party funds - they were looking to the Government which with such infinite travail they had returned to office to fulfil the pledges its members had made.

And that Government, the champions of the masses of the people of Britain - what of it? What of its members? There was Ramsay MacDonald, destined to carry on in high office for many years as Baldwin's colleague and the Tories' pet. There was Snowden, destined to ascend the ladders of orthodox finance to the House of Lords and become the pet of the Liberals. There was Thomas, destined to make money by gambling on the date of a General Election, destined to stand condemned before a tribunal for disclosing secret Cabinet information to millionaires who were even then his pals, destined to crawl snuffling from the political scene amidst the tears of the House, the pet of a decaying civilisation. And there was Oswald Mosley already the most persecuted man in British politics, destined to pass with dauntless valour through the hottest hells of persecution rather than contribute to this appalling betrayal of the people who had trusted him.

It was not to stop and dither on the brink of disaster, panic-stricken for his own career, that Mosley had cut himself adrift from the world of his birth and endured for so long the yelping of multitudinous enemies; his action in joining the Labour Party was an attempt to serve the enduring vision of a Britain reborn which he had brought back from the battlefields of France, and that vision he was determined unfalteringly to serve. He tried to jerk the Government into a sense of responsibility. He spared no pains to try and induce in Thomas the greatness to rise to the needs of the situation.

After months of unavailing effort he prepared, with the support of his colleagues, Lansbury and Johnston, a memorandum putting forward extremely important proposals to form part of a short term policy. There were to be comprehensive schemes for work of national value - land reclamation; afforestation; great roads to replace the narrow tracks that so frequently link town with town, creating obstacles for traffic and danger to life; electrification projects; everything needed to bring Britain up to date in the public utility sense; everything to equip her for survival. More important still, not only were children to be kept out of industry, but an *ad hoc* pension scheme was proposed whereby old people were to be encouraged to retire from industry at sixty by payment of a pension of 24s. a week. Thus more jobs would go to those who most urgently needed them - those on the threshold of adult life, who were growing up in idleness, and subjected to demoralisation of every kind.

This was to be only the interim programme. Mosley held that the final policy entailed nothing less than the complete reorganisation of our industrial life. The full short term policy was needed to make good adverse effects on employment which he believed to be inseparable from the processes of the transformation. By the time that British industries were rationalised, and the public works at an end, Mosley trusted that his proposals for the control of the nation's finance would have been accepted and operating to provide a high wage system for the building up of the home market, which was to be protected by an Imports Control Board making purchases in bulk. The immediate task, however, was to secure Cabinet approval for the short term policy.

The newspapers, faithful to their custom of never telling the truth when a lie would do as well, announced that the Mosley memorandum had been presented to the Cabinet behind the back of Thomas. It was represented as an attempt of Mosley's to exalt himself treacherously at his chief's expense. It so happens that it was Thomas himself who presented the memorandum to the Cabinet, together with an intimation of his own rejection of the proposals. A contradiction was issued, but it never caught up with the lie.

Thomas condemned the proposals on the ground of expense. No doubt he feared an outcry which would have united Tories and Liberals, and at this stage of his career, at least, he was not the man to go down fighting when sheer immobility alone was required to keep him at the top. Had the Labour Cabinet as a whole gone to the country with the message that they could do nothing without a clear majority, the chances are at least equal that they would have been given that majority, but even if the results turned out otherwise, they would have preserved respect for themselves and their party - a respect that they preferred to throw overboard in order to keep themselves where they were, precariously clinging to offices which cowardice prevented them from performing with vitality and drive.

Thomas made it very clear to a gratified capitalism that he disapproved of Mosley's proposals. His own policy, he said was the policy of the Government as a whole, but all this amounted to, apart from the trifling measures already noted, was a call - it could be no more than a call, mockingly echoed from the past - for expanded exports. This suited the bankers. It was, it had been for years, their favourite slogan. The newspapers began to treat Thomas with a tender sympathy. They championed him against the "absurd" crusade of Mosley, who wanted something done - as though it were the function of Government to do anything, a fallacy Baldwin had exposed so ably at the Election. The reactionary Snowden hastened to the assistance of the Lord Privy Seal. He had prepared figures to show that Mosley's pension scheme would cost £300,000,000 - a sum based on an estimate which ignored the *ad hoc* nature of the project, and made provision for the pensioning of every man over sixty independent of his income, and on the assumption of his compulsory retirement - a grotesque travesty of Mosley's idea. The scheme was to be voluntary; it was to apply only to workers. Then the great MacDonald decided to take decisive action. His decisive action was to resign from the I.L.P., which was Mosley's main centre of support!

While the Cabinet was considering his proposals - nominally, at least - Mosley concentrated upon making known his view about the need for his long-term policy of reconstruction. He spoke on the subject from innumerable platforms, and on occasion expressed a further opinion, even more significant: "It is no good expecting industry to rationalise itself unless the Government rationalises itself," he declared. "At present the Government of the country is as irrational as the organisation of industry." This was accompanied by a call to get rid of the old men as well as the old methods, an attack on the many men in politics who were senile in spirit. It was interpreted as the snarl of youth at seniors entitled to respect. "The remark does not increase our admiration for the Chancellor of the Duchy," affirmed the *Morning Post*. "The country - and the unemployed - have reason to be grateful to Mr. Thomas for refusing to aggravate the disease. If, as seems likely, he falls to the resentment of his disappointed comrades, his failure, we may be certain, will be less disastrous than their success." Thus spoke the voice of senescent Britain.

It was in other tones that Mosley spoke: "I am convinced," he told the businessmen of Smethwick, "that this country by energy and vigour in Government and in industry can within a surprisingly short space of time regain its old position at the head of the industrial nations of the world. On the other hand we cannot afford just to rely on muddling through: things will not right themselves. I have every confidence that when the Englishman knows what he is up against a great effort will be made. Our people are slow in starting and take a long time to get under way, but when they do, when they put forward their effort, they beat any other nation in the world." It was upon "muddling through," however, that the Labour Government relied.

The call of the I.L.P. group for the publication of the Mosley memorandum was rejected. It was to be regarded as "a private Cabinet Document." At a special meeting of the Parliamentary Labour Party in March of 1930 discussion of it was conveniently side-tracked after Thomas had announced that manufacturers were already finding difficulties in raising loans, and that the whole tone of finance was certainly not such as to warrant the

Government's raising many millions of money for development purposes. At this point we may recall Mosley's premonition of the previous year: "It will be little less than a disaster if in this struggle Labour support is accorded to the reactionary elements in the City. It will certainly be a fantastic negation of the purposes of our Party." Nothing was more certain than that Mosley's forebodings had been justified. The reactionary elements in the City commanded the situation, and it was not the intention of the Labour Government to dislodge them, but rather to toe the line with a policy so emasculated that it ceased to be a policy at all.

Supporters of Mosley and his two chief colleagues did their best to bring pressure to bear upon the Party pundits by mobilising the Party rank and file in Parliament. The atmosphere became heated. Snowden's Budget - another adventure in orthodoxy - did nothing to cool it down. Then came the news that the Cabinet had formally rejected the Mosley Memorandum without producing any alternative proposals. "You have got to chose between Mosley and me," Thomas was reported to have told the Premier. Whether or not that remark was actually made, it represented the real state of affairs. MacDonald chose Thomas, whose subsequent history testifies to the fact that if it is possible for a Party leader to make a wrong choice he will never fail to seize it. Almost simultaneously Thomas informed the House that the unemployment figures had risen, adding: "They are bad and getting worse. I must frankly admit that if the unemployment problem is regarded from a purely Party point of view a tremendous case can, in the light of the published figures, be made out against the Government."

That was on May 19. Next day Mosley, refusing to concur in this hateful surrender of national interests to political careerism, handed to MacDonald his resignation from the Government. It was accepted. A week later he made his speech of resignation, since become famous. Few finer speeches have ever been heard in the House.

It was made on an amendment to reduce by £100 the salaries of the Office of Lord Privy Seal moved by Baldwin. Mosley agreed that world conditions had deteriorated since the arrival of the Government in office, but insisted that this imposed upon the Government all the greater need for action. "We must be aware, as the world situation degenerates, that we do not make that situation an excuse for doing less rather than a spur for doing more." He went on to describe the differences outstanding between the Government and himself. The first concerned the question of the actual machinery employed in dealing with the problem. The existing administrative procedure resulted in most initiative coming from the Department, instead of from the Minister. He paid a sincere tribute to the Civil Service, but maintained that it was absolutely necessary that the whole initiative and drive should rest in the hands of the Government. To that end he advocated a central organisation armed with an adequate research and economic advisory department, linked to an executive machine composed of some twelve high officials, operating under the direct control of the Prime Minister and the head of the Civil Service himself, and drawing out from that central organisation the energy and initiative of the Government through every department that had to deal with the problem. He had been told that this would mean a revolution in the machinery of government, and while he was not tied to the exact details of his own scheme, he declared that some such revolution was a necessity of the times.

Mosley went on to deal with the hopes which the Government pinned to rationalisation. He affirmed the need for the reorganisation and re-equipment of industry, but quoted figures to show the displacement of labour which rationalisation entailed, thereby pointing out the moral that in itself rationalisation was no short and easy cut to the solution of the unemployment problem. He then dealt with the emphasis thrown by the Government on rationalisation in its bearing on the export trade, proving by statistics that even if the whole of that trade were to be recaptured by this means the claims of a million people entering the labour market for the first time during the next four years would not be satisfied thereby, and the situation would remain substantially the same. That was granting the Government its entire postulate, but the postulate itself was fantastic. Mosley hammered home the point that the hope of recovering our position through an expansion of our export trade was a dangerous illusion, and that the sooner the fallacy was realised the sooner would they be able to devote themselves to a search for the real remedy. He referred to the factors militating against appreciable increase in exports, stressing the industrialisation of other countries to produce for their own home markets, especially of countries which recently had no industries at all. "Take the position of our cotton trade on the Indian market," he said. "The market averaged for many years about 5,600,000,000 yards of cotton a year. That was originally our exclusive market, but today India herself produces 1,000,000,000 yards, while Japan, which only had one five-hundredth part of that Indian market, today has one fifth. The intensified competition all over the world is making more and more illusory the belief that we can again build up in the world that unique position which we occupied many years ago."

Mosley went as far as to attack some of the principles of export trade. Admitting that goods which could not be produced or grown here had to be purchased by exports, he asserted that there was no need to build up a favourable trade balance of £100,000,000 a year, or to pay for the import of the many manufactured luxury article which were pouring into the country. The solution lay in the expansion of the home market, which course he had always advocated. How could the home market be developed? Neither by *laissez-faire* nor by protection. In a striking passage he dismissed both these issues as irrelevant to modern problems. "After all," he asked, "what are the facts we have to face? We have to face fluctuations in the price level of basic commodities greater than we dreamt of before the war, for a variety of reasons, partly monetary, but still more the merging of great producers' organisations which have turned the struggle into a battle of giants in place of the day to day struggle of small merchants before the war. We have the struggle of these great organisations, and in the event of the collapse of one of them you have a downward rush in prices, or, in the event of their combination, you have an upward surge in prices which would frustrate and baffle any tariff wall that the wit of man could devise. Tariffs lead to the same fluctuations at higher price levels, while the organised and subsidised dumping that we are likely to meet in the not distant future can go over, or under, if the nation doing it so desires, or if the producers' organisations so desire, any tariff barrier that was ever invented."

The solution, claimed Mosley, who had not yet arrived at his full policy of insulation, was the system of an import control board. Applied to agriculture, and particularly to wheat, an import control board could increase the price to farmers by 10s. a quarter above the present world prices without any increase in the price of bread. Many thousands of men could thereby be found employment on the land, and he wished the policy of controlled imports to be applied no less to other trades. "If we are to build up a home market," he told the House, "it must be agreed that this nation must to some extent be insulated from the electric shock of present world conditions. You cannot build a higher civilisation and a standard of life which can absorb the great force of modern production if you are subject to price fluctuations from the rest of the world which dislocate your industry at every turn, and to the sport of competition from virtually slave conditions in other countries."

No more searching analysis of the economic situation had ever been presented to Parliament. Even Mosley's most violent antagonists were impressed, and he seized the occasion to rub home the earlier moral: "These things should be the subject of consideration and research by the most powerful economic machine that the country can devise. That is the point of my request at the beginning of my speech for a Government machine for governmental thinking."

Mosley went on to submit that the banking machinery of the century was not equipped for the task of reorganising our industrial markets. It had backed many losers; it was committed up to the hilt by many bad debts, and its ill timed generosity on occasions had assisted in the promotion and bolstering up of inefficiency. There was a convincing case for the Government taking a more effective control of the situation. Its duty, after all, was to govern. Then he made this important observation: "The worst thing that can happen to a government is to assume responsibility without control."

Next Mosley dealt with his short term policy, setting out his proposals for giving work to 800,000 people at a relatively low cost, defending them with full authority of facts and figures which nobody could challenge. He explained in great detail his pensions at sixty scheme. He outlined the difficulties and obstructive arguments which had been flung in his path and gave them their answer. In particular, he fired a broadside into the arguments of critics who had assailed the financial aspects of his policy.

"If this loan (£100,000,000) cannot be raised," he declared, "then unemployment as an urgent and immediate problem, cannot be dealt with. If we are told that we cannot have the money, let us confess defeat honourably and honestly; let us run up the white flag of surrender." He met the familiar Churchillian argument that the money needed would be taken from productive industry, and thereby create unemployment at the other end, by affirming that this was only true if deflationary policies were continued. In that event nothing could ever be done by the Government or by Parliament; no Government had any function or any purpose. "It is a policy of surrender, of negation, by which any policy can be blocked in this country." He dealt with export capitalism: "Why is it so right and proper and desirable that capital should go overseas to equip factories to compete against us, to build roads and railways in the Argentine or in Timbuctoo, to provide employment for people in those countries while it is supposed to shake the whole basis of our financial strength if anyone dares to suggest the raising of money by the Government of this country to provide employment for the people of this country? If those views are passed without examination or challenge, the position of this country is very serious indeed. In conclusion, let me say that the situation which faces us is, of course, very serious. Everybody knows that; and perhaps those who have been in office for a short time known it even better. It is not, I confidently believe, irreparable, but I feel this from the depths of my being, that the days of muddling through are over, that this time we cannot muddle through."

Then came the great and moving conclusion of a great speech, in which the whole of Mosley's political longings for his country found superb expression. Often quoted, it must still find a place here. This is what he said:-

"This nation has to be mobilised and rallied for a tremendous effort, and who can do that except the Government of the day? If that effort is not made we may soon come to crisis, to a real crisis. I do not fear that so much, for this reason, that in a crisis this nation is always at its best. This people knows how to handle a crisis; it cools their heads and steels their nerves. What I fear much more than a sudden crisis is a long, slow crumbling through the years until we sink to the level of a Spain, a gradual paralysis beneath which all the vigour and energy of this country will succumb. You have in this country resources, skilled craftsmen among the workers, design and technique among the technicians, unknown and unequalled in any other country in the world. What a fantastic assumption it is that a nation which within the lifetime of everyone has put forth efforts of energy and vigour unequalled in the history of the world, should succumb before an economic situation such as at the present. If the situation is to be overcome, if the great powers of this country are to be rallied and mobilised for a great national effort, then the Government and Parliament must give a lead. I beg the Government tonight to give the vital forces of this country the chance that they await. I beg Parliament to give that lead."

He sat down to the thunderous applause of the House. Wrote the *Morning Post* correspondent: "The sounds of cheering in which the explanation terminated were - ominous sign - common to all three parties. The *Daily Telegraph* declared: "Here was evidence of hard work, concrete thinking, and of a real political conscience, and the House, after the soft abstractions of the Prime Minister, rejoiced to feel solid ground beneath its feet...... After today's speech no one can think of Sir Oswald Mosley as a dilettante in politics. The industrious and able man, if he keeps his health and his industry, must be regarded as a candidate, some day for the highest honours."

The House of Commons had been moved to heights of enthusiasm. In the deepening twilight of its doom, marked by Mosley's great speech as he marched forward to his destiny, it could be moved to nothing else. Its power to act had gone.

11 - The Break With Labour

During his long struggle on behalf of Labour's election pledges Mosley had a very considerable body of sympathisers among the Parliamentary rank and file. His first step was to put them to the test. At a meeting of Labour members held immediately after his resignation he moved a resolution of censure on the Government's handling of unemployment. Bidden to declare itself in the open, previous support largely evaporated. Only twenty-nine votes were cast for the resolution, and over two hundred against. The caucus had been extremely active, and faced with the certainty of incurring Ministerial displeasure, to say nothing of the displeasure of the Central Office, and with the possibility of precipitating a General Election in which they might lose their seats, the Labour members rallied to their futile Government and said goodbye to every election promise which had sent them to the House.

Mosley lost no time in lamenting this spectacle of official Labour's ineptitude and cowardice. He promptly looked outside the House for support, and with his small band of followers secured the widest possible publicity for his views, delivering speech upon speech and writing article after article to instil into his fellow countrymen a sense of the crisis which threatened them. The chief victim of his attack on the Government was neither MacDonald nor Thomas, but Philip Snowden, in whose stubborn reactionary influence he found the main cause of the Labour betrayal. He named him as the man who effectively stood in the way of every drive towards reform. And Churchill unintentionally confirmed this opinion. "To replace Snowden with Mosley," he asserted, "would be injurious to our finance. I thought the London financiers precipitate and short-sighted upon an unproved Chancellor. They will be more short-sighted if they now imagine that their interests will be served by getting rid of him."

Mosley's reputation now stood higher than ever, and although the old Press attacks continued with no diminution of abuse, the better papers did not try to conceal the admiration that was felt for him among many sections of the community. The *Yorkshire Evening News* expressed a widely held view when it wrote: "Be not deceived. Sir Oswald Mosley is a man of utter sincerity. The mischief is that politics is so often spoken of as a game, spoken of with somewhat of derision. People are apt to think that clever strategy, and not burning sincerity, dictates motives and movements. Be not deceived, I say. When Sir Oswald Mosley said he felt his position in the Government to be inconsistent with honour he meant it from his heart. He has before made great sacrifices for his faith, and will make them again."

There was now to be observed in Mosley an added confidence, and in his speeches a still greater swell and power. The reason was not far to seek. He was henceforward to trust his ideals no longer to the care of leaders who were too afraid to lead. Henceforward he was to trust to his own leadership alone, and subconscious awareness of that fact must have taken a load off his mind, being now independent of the caprices and conspiracies of the little men who had hoisted the flag of surrender to International Finance.

His policy underwent a rapid evolution. Preoccupied with the need for the building up of the home market, he now became convinced that insulation of all industries (and especially agriculture) at present exposed to the chaos of world competition, was an essential part of Imperial self-sufficiency, with absolute safeguards for the consumer. He also advocated the elimination of useless Parliamentary chatter by a special Cabinet of five ministers without portfolio, but armed with full powers to legislate for the unemployment situation.

In October he went to the annual conference of the Labour Party at Llandudno with a resolution embracing these ideas, together with the gist of the long and short term policies upon which he had split with the Labour Government. The "Conservative" caucus of the Party worked strenuously against him in favour of no policy at all, but, nevertheless, over a million votes were cast for his proposals, which were defeated by only a small majority. It was a triumph. Another triumph was that, amidst scenes of acclamation, he was elected to the National Executive, while J.H. Thomas was derisively turned out. Describing the event, John Scanlan, an observer of acute perception, has written: "Sir Oswald's vote was the biggest challenge ever delivered to the governing machine. But for the fact that the issue was regarded as a vote of confidence or no confidence in the Government, Sir Oswald's vote would have been very much bigger. Delegates who were weary of the Government's inactivity, and would have liked to show their disapproval, hesitated to show the country that they had no confidence in their leaders. Loyalty, as usual carried the day...... If the Prime Minister carried all before him when he had the platform, Sir Oswald could justly claim that once the Conference settled down to business, the tide turned completely for him.

In the Press and the Labour Movement itself the discussion now centred round the question of how long it would be before Sir Oswald became the Party leader. Even without a crash in the Party's fortunes, it was easy to see that changes must come soon. The controllers of the Labour Party, mostly old men, could not stay the inexorable march of time any more than ordinary mortals. No other leader was in sight. Mr. Wheatley was gone. Mr. Maxton had none of the pushful qualities which carry a man to leadership in Labour politics, and nobody from the trade unions showed the slightest sign of being able to take charge. Therefore, every prophet fixed on Sir Oswald as the next Party leader. Even Socialists, who had no particular love for Sir Oswald, were saying nothing could stop it. All the prophets, however, had overlooked the one man who could stop it - Sir Oswald himself."[2]

---

2   *Decline and Fall of the Labour Party.*

In December there appeared a manifesto entitled "A National Policy for National Emergency," and bearing the signatures of seventeen of Mosley's Labour supporters in the House, together with his own. It was a statement of policy based upon his now familiar proposals for dealing with crisis, and included the headings "Parliament" (the Emergency Cabinet), "Economic Planning (to secure an economic balance and develop the resources of the State). "Agriculture" (Import Control Board), "Manufacturing Industry" (Commodity Board to stabilise industrial conditions and safeguard the consumer), "Export Trade" (mostly Imperial development for self-sufficiency), "Housing" (including a big slum clearance scheme), "The Necessity for Action" ("the immediate question is not a question of ownership, but of the survival of British industry").

Readers interested in the charge of inconsistency so often levelled against Mosley are invited to turn back to the Harrow elections and ponder upon the extraordinary way in which every one of his primary aims came to be developed and embodied under these new heads.

The political atmosphere was now full of excitement. There was much talk of a new and more realistic alignment of parties. Llandudno encouraged Mosley to believe that a sufficiently strong body of support would be forthcoming to force through a policy of action. That is why he continued to plead for Party unity, concurrent with the vigorous advocacy of his own programme. The discontent of the Labour rank and file, both in and out of the House, ought not to express itself, he still believed in Party disintegration: what was wanted was the mobilisation of opinion to swing its executive over to the side of action. Had that happened the old leaders would, no doubt, have resisted, and the initiative would have passed to younger and abler men. There is little doubt that Mosley would have been entrusted with the lead.

Meanwhile, the leading members of the Government were looking round for help that would make their own positions more secure. They were ready to ally themselves with any side which would allow them to keep their jobs. Overtures were made to both Liberals and Conservatives. Thus began the new conspiracy that was to result in the "National" Government and the complete triumph of the forces of reaction, which were henceforward to exert a still more unchallenged sway over the country to the detriment of every national interest.

The great danger was that before their plans matured Mosley might capture the Labour Party. Although he no longer had the united support of Maxton's I.L.P. group (they preferred adherence to a purely doctrinaire Socialism that no longer had any meaning), his strength was rapidly growing all over the country and even in Parliament, where his views commanded an increasingly attentive hearing. The jeers of the old days were heard no more. While controversy raged round his latest proposals, the first intimation of official Labour's attitude towards him was given in a speech by Herbert Morrison, who could devise no better line of attack than to rehash the old Tory nonsense about his aristocratic origins. He described Mosley as a Tory Protectionist, "who still had a certain amount of true blue blood in his veins, and who will need more time to absorb the healthy democratic instincts of organised labour and be fully inspired by the real Socialist feelings of the common people." Most of the Party organs reviewed his programme in a spirit of defeatism. "As a creed which will carry the democratic Socialist Movement to new adventures it is more than sterile," declared *Forward*.

Mosley replied in a speech at Birmingham. "Our opponents," he said, "have little reasonable criticism to offer beyond the usual personal abuse and the customary gibes of the political game. Their contribution to a discussion on a national emergency is a snarl or a schoolgirl's giggle. I have not great regard for people who are content to occupy comfortable seats without the power of carrying out the policy in which they believe. Without a change in the machinery of government no policy can be carried out on a scale adequate to deal with the present situation." In an article written for the *Sunday Chronicle* he counter-attacked more vigorously:-

"The old wives of politics are at least united in their opposition to machinery for getting things done. They are the people who for years have thwarted the democratic rights of the nation in order to maintain the 'talkie' rights of the professional windbags. There is nothing in our proposals that interferes with the control of the people over public affairs. But we do propose that the will of the people should no longer be obstructed by Parliamentary obstruction ...... The industrialisation of the world raises production beyond what the markets can absorb; the increased competition causes prices to fall, the uneconomic prices impoverish the producing countries, and their impoverishment reduces their power to buy. The world is driving on to ruin in a confusion of falling prices and competitive production. Britain's vast foreign trade involves us in this ruin to a greater extent than any other country. We would certainly take every step by reorganisation to promote our export trade, but we do not believe that this alone can solve our unemployment problem.

Our policy is designed to build a large home market, and to do this it is necessary to 'insulate' this country, and to shelter our production from the full consequences of world-wide economic warfare. We cannot reduce the world to order, we can only use the power of persuasion. In our home market we have the power to plan; to organise the full exploitation of the resources under our control; to employ our surplus labour in the reconstruction of British industry in harmony with the changed conditions. In that task we can be helped by close co-operation with the other countries in the British Commonwealth, who are linked to us by ties of sentiment; whose production is largely complementary rather than competitive; and whose economic interest can also be served by reciprocal trading arrangements, and the assured stable markets which can be secured for them and for us as a result of organisation and planning. It is not surprising that our policy encounters opposition. We do not promise a comfortable journey into the land of plenty. We summon the country to a greater effort than ever before. We do not believe that prosperity will return to this country like the sun appearing from behind a cloud. For ten years the complacency of the incompetent has kept us drifting to slow disaster. We live in an age of change which demands action." J.L. Garvin, to whom it has so often been given to catch a glimpse of great truths, summed up the Mosley crusade in this fine passage:-

"It would be easy to overwhelm the Mosley manifesto with objections in detail. But its merit lies in its unflinching recognition that without a national awakening to the necessity for 'peace-energy on a war-scale' - as we put it long ago - the Empire cannot be maintained and Britain's traditional greatness in the world cannot endure. Sir Oswald Mosley himself has taken his political life in his hands with brilliant fearlessness. He is the only leader of his generation who has the courage to strike out a new path, even though it may lead him temporarily into the wilderness. He and his friends, as pioneers in the Labour Party, appeal primarily to the mass of Labour. We are less interested in that than in the general national effect. The result of the violent discussion certain to ensue will be to compel conventional politicians in every party to face 'the pain of a new idea.' The spirit of the thing is more than the letter. Britain can only wither by trying to live on the old roots. All who reject Mosley's idea of fundamental reform in method and purpose, must produce alternatives as bold."

The difference of approach to national problems between Mosley and the doctrinaire Socialists was admirably demonstrated in the Commons when Lansbury informed the House that international Socialism was the only cure for the country's ills, and when Mosley asked, not without derision, whether Britain had to wait until Socialism came to Timbuctoo. On another occasion he attacked the Labour principle of the "inevitability of gradualness." It might well be, he said, that gradualness was the best method when we had time to be gradual, but "when we are falling downstairs, bumping from step to step, it is no good saying that it is better to go gradually."

Mosley soon made up his mind that no further efforts could avail to turn the Labour Party into an instrument of the people's will. It had become too firmly established as a vested interest. Although he had devoted to the cause several strenuous years of his life; although its highest positions were still open to him if he could but consent to play the Party game, he decided that its foundations were too rotten to permit of the erection of any worthy superstructure. He was convinced that entirely new foundations had to be laid, and towards that task he now set his face. First, he delivered a lacerating attack on the Government from the floor of the House. He denounced them for having no constructive policy. "At this moment," he declared, "the Prime Minister's complacency is perhaps one of the most serious dangers that face the country. If he could descend for a moment from contemplation and complacency, the business of this country might proceed more rapidly." Then he turned his attention to Snowden, reiterating the charge that the rentier class was his pampered darling, affirming that his call for "sacrifice for all" (which was his only suggestion for meeting the impending financial crisis) was the suggestion of an old woman in fright, and demanding a complete reversal of the policy under which Mr. Snowden, before agreeing to any expenditure, must first see worked every detail of a scheme at a great cost of money and departmental energy. He concluded upon a characteristic note of challenge: "We have had a long hymn of fatuous optimism, when every one of those who took a more serious view of the national situation was mocked and derided by the Government. Suddenly they wake up with a bang to the facts of national crisis. Even then they have no plan. This is another case of men who cannot see danger until it hits them in the face - and then they lose their heads. They are like chickens running in front of a motor car and cackling the economy slogans of their opponents. These suggestions to put the nation in bed on a starvation diet!

These are suggestions of old men in a fright. The exact reverse is needed - a policy of manhood which takes the nation out into the fields, which builds up the muscle and the constitution by effort."

The secession from Labour of Mosley's group began with letters of resignation sent to the Premier by John Strachey and Dr. Robert Forgan. Oliver Baldwin, W.J. Brown, and Lady Cynthia followed, Brown affirming that he did not propose to join any other organisation. Unfortunately, Mosley himself fell ill with pleurisy at this stage, and while he was on his sick-bed the National Executive went through the solemn and redundant farce of expelling him from the Party, after he had in fact, launched his New Party.

Premises had previously been taken by the group in Great George Street, and it was here that the New Party was launched upon its short and not very happy career. Mosley had resolved to give the party system one last trial. He had suffered first-hand experience of other parties and their leaders. He knew that nothing was to be expected from them in the way of a policy to place Britain again on its feet. He thought it just possible that a new party, advancing his own policy that had everywhere received an enthusiastic support from audiences, would meet with some chance of electoral success, if only the people were fully alive to the seriousness of the crisis. There were a large number of Members of Parliament who shared that view, not only among Labour men, but among Conservatives and Liberals as well. At first it seemed likely that they would join the New Party; several had definitely undertaken to do so. But when the critical moment arrived, with the exception of the tiny Labour group and one brilliant young Conservative, W.E.D. Allen, they all drew back and preferred to pursue the line of least resistance, abandoning a policy which they knew was necessary for the country's salvation. They performed a public service in thus making clear at the outset that the people of Britain could not look to even the "advanced" members of the old gangs for that high courage, determination, and self-sacrifice which alone could deal with the most formidable tasks which were lying ahead - tasks more tremendous than any body of men or women had ever been called upon to shoulder in British political history.

12 - An Epic of Defeat

There can be no doubt that what adversely affected the morale of Labour and other members who believed in the New Party policy, but refused to work for it, was something more than the political precariousness of the struggle - something that might not be unfairly described as panic at the thought of the physical violence that the new venture would have to endure. The Labour Party had not for decades been obliged to cope with this violence, because the violence was almost entirely enlisted on its behalf. Its politicians were accustomed to acclamation wherever they went to speak, and when opposition meetings were broken up, and opposition speakers assaulted, they had the comforting knowledge that they themselves were on the side of the angels - or, at any rate, on the side of the thugs. No such fortune was to attend the New Party, for reasons which must here be analysed and explained.

For years past the masses had been accustomed to think of the Labour Party as the sole repository of their hopes, and not lightly would they give up that touching and pathetic faith. MacDonald and Snowden and Thomas were still their heroes, and when disillusionment came, when these men could conceal no longer that they had made their peace with the enemy, their actions were taken as purely personal defections, in no way casting a reproach upon the incorruptible Labour Party, so that the only thing necessary was to transfer their wholehearted trust to the next bunch of leaders on the list, Lansbury, Atlee, Morrison, and the rest, convinced that, although the first bunch had failed lamentably, the second would infallibly succeed in securing for them the square deal which is their due. Only today, after six strenuous years spent by Mosley in opening their eyes to the true position, are they beginning to see that it is quite impossible for any party to remain uncorrupted which tries to work a system that places supreme power, not in Westminster, but in the City of London.

It is natural that there should have been this time lag between fact and perception of the fact by the British people. The Labour Government had not possessed an absolute majority in Parliament, so that it was easy for the heroes of that Government to tell their devoted followers that they would have been "most bloody, bold, and resolute" had their voting power given them complete control. Even if their subsequent marriage with the Tories made this seem a little dubious in retrospect, the people could still bring themselves to believe that the Labour Party was the chosen instrument of destiny, and that an Atlee or a Lansbury would have used an absolute majority to deal faithfully with the bankers and monopolists, and to usher into existence the long-promised "new and better order."

Since the mass of Labour Supporters did not at that time recognise that the Labour Party was as much a racket as the Tory party, it was not difficult for the caucus to persuade them that Mosley, in abandoning it, had proved himself a traitor to their cause. They had built up the Party and it was sacred to them. They forgot that they had applauded Mosley's sincerity when he threw over his Government office on behalf of the programme for which they had voted. They forgot that subsequently they had given him a rapturous welcome when he came among them to enlist their support for the proposals which he had drawn up for furthering that programme. They took no account of the virtual certainty that he had abandoned the Labour Party for the same reason that he had abandoned the Labour Government - because it was worse than useless for every purpose for which adherence to the Labour programme entailed. Their one thought was that Labour was their citadel and that Mosley had left it to its own devices. They now remembered the innumerable jibes which the newspapers had made about Mosley's wealth and title; the incessant sneers which they had cast upon what they described as his "Socialist" pose; their incessant cry that it was impossible for a wealthy aristocrat to possess any genuine desire to help the under-dog at the expense of his own class. Had the people been in a position to sense the atmosphere of cowardice and shuffling expediency which disgraced the Government, or the fatuous discontent and sterile opportunism of the Labour back-benches, it is certain that they would never have cast a single doubt on Mosley's adamantine devotion to their own true interests. As they were not in that position they surged forward to smash his meetings and seek opportunities to do him a physical injury.

The first hints of the new persecution came from Smethwick and Stoke-on-Trent, where the caucus had been busy pulling strings among the local Party officials. Mosley being seriously ill with pleurisy, Lady Cynthia took the lead in explaining the motives behind their break from Labour. Displaying a courage which should have put the halting, democratic pseudo-sympathisers to shame, this magnificent woman went to Stoke-on-Trent to face her constituents. She was noisily received. They demanded her resignation. She rounded on her critics, rebuking them for what she described as their "check and humbug." She told her audience that she had kept faith with them in supporting the programme which she had been returned to the House to support. If there had been betrayal it certainly did not lie at her door. If resignation were demanded they should not approach her, but the Labour Front Bench. So clearly and convincingly did she put her case that much potential hostility was allayed and many firm friends retained. Then she went to address big meetings at Manchester, Dundee, Liverpool, Leeds, and Newcastle, where there was still more sound and fury and where she had the mortification of hearing hurled at her from her former supporters all those old insults about her wealth and position which they had learnt from the Yellow Press. She did not flinch from the ordeal, but counter-attacked and made good her position in the minds of every reasonable man and woman present.

Another big meeting, held in London, established the fact that the opposition was being carefully organised and that official

Labour was now as keen to hound Mosley out of the political arena as the Tories had ever been, even in the days when they had raged the most. The Labour leaders knew, among other things, how utterly Mosley had "got their measure" and there was little they would not do to frustrate his exposure of their venality and worthlessness.

The great capitalist newspapers and weekly and monthly journals which for so long had subjected the Labour Party to a sustained bombardment, now accorded space and guineas to every Labour opportunist and hack who wished to get even with Mosley for his honesty. There was no misrepresentation too absurd to find its way into print. Because he advocated Imperial insulation for the safeguarding of the home market, they declared that he was in league with Beaverbrook. Because Morris (now Lord Nuffield) agreed with his proposals for the rehabilitation of British industry, they hinted that he had become the hireling of capitalism. Because he denied the possibility of real recovery upon a free trade basis, they said that he was angling to rejoin the Conservative Party. They even went so far in their fury as to deny him all personal charm - a quaint libel to anyone who knows Mosley. And, of course, they put their little minds through each stage of what they were pleased to describe as his "careerism," which was the most dishonest charge they could have brought against him. The man who forgoes every social and political advantage of his position by his refusal to compromise, who later declines the ascent of the Cabinet ladder in order not to violate his own principles, and who finally cuts himself adrift from a Party in which he had immense influence and prestige to face the extraordinary difficulties of fashioning his own instrument - such a man is not of the stuff of which careerists are made. But the qualities of a Mosley are so rarely encountered in the shiftless democratic world that the average run of politicians is quite unable to believe in them, and, therefore, they attributed his rejection of accepted ruts to an impatient desire to short-circuit the spiral of advancement in order to arrive more quickly at fame and power. That this view is moonshine only a few minutes' quiet reflection will establish. Had he been but one among the many political opportunists of the day he would have stayed with the Tories, where his abilities would have placed him head and shoulders above those of its young men who are now so widely boosted - its Edens and Duff Coopers, and the rest. He would certainly have stayed with the Labour Party, where his eminence was vastly greater than that of Lansbury or Attlee, so that today he would almost inevitably have been the Labour alternative for the Premiership. The suggestion that he broke with these Parties because of personal ambition can only be supported on the theory that Mosley is a fool - and not even his worst enemies have the audacity to suggest that. Therefore, reasonable people are driven back to the position of accepting his impatience at its face value, as the imperious desire for action of a great patriot confronting the facts of national crisis and decline which everywhere else are accepted with complacency - a patriot rapidly becoming conscious that the revolutionary changes demanded by the times could not be carried out under the existing system even if he had the control.

It soon became clear to Mosley that even more was required than an entirely new political party, since it proved impossible - so long as the old Party tradition was followed - to legislate against internal disruption and squabbling. The local committee principle had been retained by the New Party, which led to every difference as to method being magnified by the usual interminable discussions and cross-purposes. The social-democrats who had nerved themselves to follow Mosley into the new organisation felt ill at ease with their own boldness, and that gave a neurotic tinge to the atmosphere. Moreover, the pompous egotism of local pundits soon resulted in typical complaints about their "not having been consulted," about this, that, or the other thing. This happened, in fact, in the middle of an important campaign, when every adherent should have had the grace to leave his own pet vanities at home. A vacancy having occurred at Ashton-under-Lyne, the New Party decided to make a bid for the seat with Allan Young, their brilliant organising secretary, as the candidate.

The consequence was that while the fight raged the Manchester executive of the Party resigned in a body, for reasons which their spokesman announced to the Press. Describing a conference at which the matter was discussed, he said: "I pointed out - and here is an important point - that we had never been consulted about the possibility of a candidate in the Ashton election, although it is only a few miles away. The members who had done the work had not been considered, or their opinion even sounded, in the matter of nominating candidates." So they threw in their hands. These were the men who rallied to their country in the hour of political crisis, now throwing away their cause because it had not been thought necessary to invite them to debate the pros and cons of an election outside their own constituency. The truth behind the revolt was that the spokesman had been refused a paid job. No wonder Mosley came to the conclusion that the democratic spirit carries with it the ardour of its own decay!

The Ashton election was a hard tussle. Greenwood, Minister of Health, announced official Labour's injunction to "trample the New Party underfoot. In every constituency where it raises its head we shall do battle." Other speakers trotted out the old stuff about the Mosleys on the Riviera. Ramsay MacDonald entered the battle to rally the Labour forces against Mosley. "Politics," he said, "is like football in this - that unless you play as a team, fight as a team, pass as a team, you will never do anything." True enough, but what of the team that stands in such awe of the other side that it never attacks, never tries to score goals at their expense, and even, in an excess of good nature, turns round and scores for its opponents? Would any footballer worthy of the name retain a place in that team? Tom Johnston, one of Mosley's colleagues in dealing with unemployment, who had stayed on to make his peace with the Government and to become Lord Privy Seal when Thomas bolted to the Dominions Office, arrived on the scene to suggest that sinister powers were financing Mosley in an attempt to wreck the Labour Party.

Mosley, now restored to health, put up a great battle on behalf of the New Party candidate. Attacking MacDonald's "gradualism," he said: "I refuse to wait until every negro, every savage in every quarter of the world has been organised, his wages raised, his standards lifted, and until the dumping of the products of sweated labour shall have ceased. Must the workers of Ashton wait until every Hottentot has learned to call Mr. Henderson 'Comrade' at Geneva?"

A member of his audience taxed him with dictatorship ambitions, to which he retorted: "Where's the poor boob in this country who thinks he's got democracy? Democracy means carrying out the will of the people. When has that been done?"

And then, answering Johnston, Mosley exploded a bomb under the Labour Party by revealing the existence of secret Labour funds contributed by rich men, chief among whom was the late Bernhard Baron, the Jewish tobacco millionaire. The Labour hierarchy was stricken with dismay at this subtle counter-thrust, since the public had not previously been aware of these sources of income owned by a Party that had consistently attacked the secret Party funds of others. The move was represented to the workers as another piece of Mosley's treachery against them.

The gallant fight for the seat was reflected but decisively in the figures. Only four thousand votes were cast for Young, and these opened the door for the Conservative to squeeze home. Labour supporters were furious. Their belief in their Party still persisting, twenty thousand of them gathered to make a hostile demonstration against Mosley, whom police escorted through ranks hissing and yelling the word "traitor." He faced them with a smile, and endeavoured unsuccessfully to address them. Allan Young had to be smuggled away from the Town Hall by a back door.

The New Party not long afterwards was subjected to further processes of disintegration. Allan Young resigned. He had given fine and constructive services to the Mosley movement, but, unfortunately, he was not nervously adjusted to all the rancour and hatred which the new movement had to endure. An extremely able, sincere man, he retired from the scene to work as constructively as possible among men whose challenge and tempo made less demands upon his nervous energy. John Strachey, Mosley's chief lieutenant, also found the passage rather too rough for his temperament. Brilliantly intellectual, he was not the man of action type. He did not thrive upon violent hostility. From the first he had no great heart for the New Party adventure, and in its subsequent development he would have been quite out of place. His pretext for the break was that Mosley's policy of Imperial self-sufficiency put the Empire above Russia, and now he is perfectly happy among the Reds, attacking Mosley at the latter's great overflow meetings as an official Communist speaker.

Mosley, Cynthia Mosley, Forgan, and W.E.D. Allen - these alone remained of the Parliamentary secessionists, and they went forward, refusing to be dismayed. The Press was loudly announcing the extinction of their cause. The Labour Party were rabid for revenge. The valiant little group proceeded to make their dispositions for the General Election, at which their fortunes were to sink to almost nothingness.

What precipitated the retreat of many of the democrats from the New Party ranks was the fact that Mosley was determined not to allow his meetings to be smashed by hooligans spurred on by the Labour and Communist Parties. Violence was increasing and threatened to make impossible the holding of meetings, just as it had previously driven many Conservatives away from towns where the hooligan element was particularly strong. Many of Mosley's supporters would have been well content if he had followed the example of the Tories and declined to show the New Party nose in districts where hostility lay in wait for it. But that did not square with his own spirit. Meetings addressed by Lady Cynthia during his illness had been wrecked by organised bands of rowdies: evidence was plentiful that still greater violence was being planned. "We are going to defend the right of free speech in this country," declared Mosley. "We will not tamely submit to intimidation and ruffianism." Among his followers were many splendid young Britons who passionately shared his vision of a national rebirth, and these he formed into a Youth Movement providing facilities for boxing and physical exercise. One of the functions of this group was to steward meetings and to meet force with force, using no weapon but only the "good old British fist" in order to secure a hearing for the Party speakers. Half the Press was derisive - the "Biff Boys" was the term with which they described the young men. The other half was indignant and alarmed. "Hitlerian Storm Troops," "Mosley's Army," "Mosley's Thugs" figured prominently in the headlines, as though it were a wicked thing to deny sub-human Yahoos the right to smash up meetings as they chose. There was now heard the swift patter of feet as the Social Democrats ran away from Mosley's iron resolve to face violence whenever and wherever it presented itself. In this virile atmosphere there seemed to be no place for them and away they scampered; among them the Lib.-Lab. philosopher, C.E.M. Joad, shouting over his shoulder as he ran, how much he detested "the cloven hoof of Fascism."

Meanwhile, the Parliamentary attack continued unabated. When the Unemployment Insurance (Anomalies) Bill came before the House, the New Party group vigorously opposed it on the ground that it would withdraw still more purchasing power from the people and was, therefore, worse than useless as an alternative to robust legislation setting the unemployed to work. Turning to the Government Benches, Mosley remarked, with withering scorn: "By this measure you buy until the autumn another short lease of your own miserable lives. You buy it at the expense of the poorest of your supporters who voted for you at the last election, and you buy it at the expense of British industry, which your continuance in office places in increasing jeopardy. It is a tribute to the strength and vitality of the country that, under these handicaps, it can still continue to look forward, not without some hope, in the not too-distant future to the emergence of some force and policy."

Next came the reshuffle whereby MacDonald and Baldwin were to prove that the difference supposed to be outstanding between their two Parties had no basis in fact. The reshuffle was brought into being by the so-called "economic blizzard." Snowden decided that it had to be met at the expense of the already impoverished purchasing power of the people by means of the Means Test and other noxious economy measures. Most of the proposed cuts received the support of the present Labour leaders, as was later confirmed by many in a position to know, and notably by Mr. J. McGovern, who declared: "I can, outside this House, on any platform...... enter into discussion and debate...... and show that the Labour Party in debate in this House have always accepted every form of Means Test, that the majority of the (Labour) Cabinet accepted the whole of the cuts that took place under the late Labour Government, and that since that time they have shuffled without end in attempting to put the blame on other persons... At the Scarborough Conference the Hon. Member for Dumbarton Burghs (Mr. Kirkwood) moved against the Means Test, and Tom Johnston, the late Lord Privy Seal, moved the application of a Means Test, but not on a Poor Law basis - whatever that means. The motion was carried overwhelmingly by the Labour Conference that a Means Test be applied to the workers of this country in receipt of transitional benefit... The Labour Party not only agreed with the Means Test, but the majority of the Party agreed with the cuts." Nevertheless, when the T.U.C. made its opinion known in very decided terms, these leaders had no compunction in turning to rend the very proposals to which they had given their support only a few days previously.

When the Coalition came, MacDonald, Snowden, Thomas, and other doughty champions of the working man linked arms with the champions of the bankers to the mutual benefit of everybody except the British nation and those Labour leaders who could not be accommodated with ministerial jobs and were therefore disposed to perceive the wisdom of listening to the T.U.C. "The Labour Party is dead! Long live the Labour Party!" might well have been their motto. Months before, this hopeless institution had shown that its inertia and lack of principle were shared by all its members, but when the senior leaders by their actions exposed the sham of maintaining that there was any real hiatus between Labour and Tory policies, the junior leaders, their noses out of joint, saw the opportunity to curry favour as the new guardians of the Party and the new champions of the masses. Their future leader, Lansbury, led the charge on the Means Test against all comers. These fresh histrionics and new alignments of humbug captured the interest of the electors, so that the issues were lost in a riot of confusion, and relatively few people kept their minds on the only practical proposals that had been advanced for Britain's recovery - the proposals of Mosley and his New Party followers.

Mosley at once discerned that the new Coalition was simply an expedient whereby the Labour seniors might keep themselves in power by serving the bankers through further attacks on the standard of living of the people. His criticism was pungent. "The New Party," he announced, "will oppose any reduction in the standard of life of the working classes. They are ready to apply their published policy to safeguard the home market. I do not think the present Government can be called a National Government, because I do not believe the nation supports a Government composed of men who have failed conspicuously in the past, who have been driven like sheep before the present crisis and are now huddled in one corner of the pen. It is a Government of united 'muttons'."

The New Party was now publishing a weekly paper bearing the admirable name *Action*. Unfortunately even this did not prosper as it should have done. Its staff was recruited on anything but a sacrificial basis and lacked the particular drive and spirit which alone could give Mosley the strong support that he needed. The journal was a democratic hotchpotch, containing a little of everything, futilely designed to tackle every palate. Its editor, Harold Nicholson, seemed to think that the most useful contribution he could make towards a new political and economic order in Britain was the writing and featuring of book reviews which more often than not had nothing to do with either politics or economics.

Branches of the New Party were established in many parts of the country, but here again the vicious undermining of the spirit of action by talk hampered the movement. "We have suffered throughout," wrote Mosley, "from the activities of those who delighted in the discussion of theory on every subject and have impeded us in the hard and practical work of organisation." So far as possible organisational difficulties were overcome and mistakes rectified, and so far as possible the idea of voluntary discipline was instilled into members, but the need for rapid improvisation left the Party at the mercy of many disintegrating factors, chief of which was this cursed love of talk of a host of supporters. Most of them had come from the older parties, where they seemed to have been encouraged to hold forth at great length about every detail on which they had disagreed with method or policy, thereby inhibiting the progress of either. Mosley did his best with much impossible material. He cut out chairman and platform supporters and votes of thanks and other conventional nonsense at meetings, each principal speaker appearing alone and handling the proceedings without support. He tried to create a spirit alien to political parties - the spirit of getting on with the job and sacrificing all pretensions of the ego in order to do that job more efficiently: the spirit of service and self-sacrifice to the cause. But men who have reached maturity encased in hard-boiled egotism and given to fussy self-assertions are not easily to be tempted out of their old habits into the perceptions of a sterner, more exacting need. Recruits came and went. There was a flux and change from the first days of the Party to the last. Only a man of Mosley's iron determination could have kept it together for a sufficient length of time to be remorselessly floored at the polls.

The New Party decided to contest twenty-three seats. Cynthia Mosley, not being in good health, Mosley decided to fight her constituency, Stoke-on-Trent, in his own Staffordshire. He had some very successful meetings there, but elsewhere the persistent barrage of misrepresentation had its effect, and most of his candidates found themselves swamped by torrents of hatred. Mosley himself was rushed by a wild mob at Birmingham. The meeting was held at the Rag Market, and had not been in progress long when the stewards were called into action. Fighting broke out in every part of the hall. Several New Party officials were injured, and some carried out unconscious, streaming with blood. Mosley went down from the platform to try and restore order. Chairs were seized and used as weapons against him and his colleagues, and there was a mad rush to try and wreck the platform. The meeting ended in the most amazing disorder. Outside in the street a huge mob had gathered, and Mosley proposed to exercise the right of every Englishman to walk along the road to his hotel. He was threatened with arrest by the police if he did not immediately enter a car, so convinced were they of the danger to his life. Mosley held out and was eventually accompanied from the scene on foot. A comic sequel to the meeting was that it was Mosley who was summoned for assault, the opposition faking a charge of kicking a man with his right foot - which they did not know had been incapacitated for such purposes by his war injury. It was contemptuously dismissed by the Bench.

Two evenings later there was more rowdyism when Mosley addressed meetings in Glasgow, one in the open air and another, where the crowd smashed the doors of the hall. He was struck by a bottle, and his supporters were attacked with razors. Several "National" candidates, subjected to the same kind of violence, promptly surrendered by cancelling their meetings, as they have done on many occasions since. This was not Mosley's way. A day or two later at Glasgow police in great numbers attended another of his meetings, and the crowd demanded that they should be withdrawn, Mosley replied that he had not invited the police, and had no control over them, whereupon the audience rose in a body and left in an ugly frame of mind. To their amazement they found that Mosley had followed them outside, and that he proposed to address them entirely on his own, without any support. In admiration of his courage they gave him a fair hearing. Something of the grandeur of the man stirred the imagination of other audiences. There was a marvellous gathering in the Manchester Free Trade Hall, of which the *Manchester Guardian* wrote: "In his thirty-fifth year Oswald Mosley is already thickly crusted with legend. His disposition and his face are those of a raider, a corsair; and his place in the history of these times will be won, if at all, with the sword. We speak metaphorically; but who could doubt when Oswald Mosley sat down after his speech on Saturday, and the audience, stirred as an audience rarely is, rose and swept a storm of applause towards the platform - who could doubt that here was one of those root-and-branch men who have been thrown up from time to time in the religious, political, and business story of England...... his ideas swept a great audience off its feet, and the scene at the end was matter for thought to any 'elder statesman.'"

For the most part, however, Mosley's ideas were not given a chance, being shouted down time after time by the mob. At Fenton a brick missed him by inches and his chauffeur was knocked down and kicked. There were dozens of similar incidents. The ape-men were in command, and not all Mosley's great-hearted efforts could keep the ring for reason. His physical courage had proved as immense as his intellectual courage, but he could not turn the tide. Howled down, kicked, abused, misrepresented, every one of his candidates failed at the polls. Mosley secured ten thousand votes to take third place at Stoke. Most of the others lost their deposits. Once again the Old Gang had played the trump-card of national peril, and with it they won all along the line. The Coalition heroes were sent to Westminster in great numbers to keep the pound on gold, and three months later they sought congratulations on being driven off the Gold Standard. Labour itself lost two hundred and thirty-eight seats.

The big interests breathed freely for the first time for many a day, not so much because of the defeat of Labour, as because of what had happened to this man Mosley. From such a catastrophic defeat he could never again rise; such was their conviction. And there was another patter of feet as the last remaining democrats rushed from his side.

"Exit New Party" was the favourite headline in the Press. Mosley's own thoughts ran along a different line. Writing in the last issue of the old *Action* he declared:

"Better the great adventure, better the great attempt for England's sake, better defeat, disaster, better far the end of that trivial thing called a political career than stifling in the uniform of blue and gold, strutting and posturing on the stage of Little England, amid the scenery of decadence, until history in turning over an heroic page of the human story writes of us the contemptuous postscript: 'These were the men to whom was entrusted the Empire of Great Britain, and whose idleness, ignorance, and cowardice left it a Spain.' We shall win; or at least we shall return upon our shields."

13 - Birth of British Fascism

The New Party defeat would have broken the heart of a lesser man and smashed his career. Mosley rose from the wreckage of his hopes, not only unbroken, but stronger, more determined, more utterly devoted to his cause than ever in the past. While shouts of derision were being encountered on all sides, while the political and newspaper sub-men were debating whether he would be allowed to crawl back into the Conservative or Labour ranks, he was planning the greatest adventure of his career, and the boldest move in the history of British politics.

Mosley does not look upon the New Party experience as a mistake, in the sense that Hitler regards his Putsch as a mistake. It was a disaster necessary to prove the utter bankruptcy of the Party method as a means to revitalise a great nation. He had seen how his "New Members' Association" of 1918, had been wafted out of existence by the simple magic of social intercourse and flattery. He had seen, to his infinite sorrow, how the same magic had destroyed the challenge of Labour, whose adherents had been dined and wined and corrupted by all the prizes that the old world had to offer. He had seen how even an honest man like Maxton had been cunningly robbed of his sting and danger by capitalism's device of painting him as a picturesque revolutionary and "good fellow." He now saw that any new Party that was merely political must attract to itself men brought up in the corrupt atmosphere of the old Parties - mostly political failures who had more talk than action to contribute, more egotism than service, more pomposity than guts. What was needed, he now realised with intense conviction, was a great new movement of new men and new methods - a surging, passionate movement, not of Party wrangling and expediency-mongering, but of spiritual rebirth. An instrument had to be forged for service to the people's will, an instrument of iron that would withstand the united resistance of old world violence, misrepresentations, lies and seductions, an instrument with which the British nation might cut through the tangled undergrowth of decadence, put an end to the system of plunder, and drive out humbug in order to face up to its problems with courage and build bravely for the future, instead of allowing financial brigands and political coxcombs to bring about its ruin by their incompetence and greed. It would be a movement of the finest men and women of the British race, dedicated to long years of toil, sacrifice, and bitter disappointments, prepared and organised to face violence and even death, surrendering every fussy claim of the ego and bidding farewell to creature comforts in order that their nation and their Empire might survive and again take first place in the vanguard of the mighty peoples of the world.

Such a movement, being devotedly loyal to the Crown, would have to organise constitutionally in order to achieve political power. But that would be its only association with politics. Proud, hard, resistant, it would secure return of specifically selected members to Parliament, not to become absorbed in its vitiating atmosphere, but to drive back into obscurity those whom the atmosphere had poisoned, to take charge of Britain and organise a great corporate system which would enable the people to rule in their own country and outlaw the brigands and the parasites who are its present masters and who have damnably betrayed their masterdom. It would be a movement of discipline and relentless purpose, refusing all compromise with the old world, brooking no opposition in power save the constructive criticism of technicians as to ways and means, restoring to the land the heroic and historic principle of leadership, and marching forward to the attainment of a civilisation in keeping with the immortal spirit of the million men who died that Britain might live - and live to great purposes.

Thus entirely by his own thought and experience did Mosley arrive at the modern concept of life known as Fascism or National Socialism. He did not lose time blanching at names which the racketeers of financial democracy for years had heralded throughout Britain as synonymous with wickedness, and, indeed, with the grossest depravity. He went first to Italy and then to Germany - to learn.

In Italy, where there had been no such facade of respectability as that behind which vested interests cloak their aims in Britain, and where the people were less susceptible to the dope of meaningless catchwords, the system of Financial Democracy had broken down very much sooner - indeed, it occurred immediately after the War. In that breakdown the real nature and logic of democracy were shown up in all their inherent absurdities. Every political and economic faction fought for its own hand. Where labour was plentiful the employers emerged as petty tyrants; where it was scarce the Trade Union leaders assumed the tyrant's mantle and imposed impossible terms. There were vast strikes and lock-outs every day of the week. Trains arriving within even twelve hours of time were rare phenomena. To post a letter was a gamble as to the likelihood of its receipt; to post a parcel was to make a certain present to someone other than the intended recipient. Gas and electricity and water were cut off whenever caprice might dictate; roads were dug up and left unrepaired for months; trams were abandoned in the street. The national life had almost ceased to function. There was fighting and bloodshed: ex-servicemen were stoned; mob hysteria dominated the scene. Neither Reactionary nor Red had the courage to take charge and govern the mob. Italy was falling rapidly to pieces in a welter of democratic brigandage. Out of this agony of a great people's exhaustion emerged Fascism - the force that has integrated the modern world and saved it from collapse. Mussolini, one of the superlatively great leaders of mankind, organised his Blackshirts to take the Italian rabble by the throat and shake it into a sense of self-discipline and self-respect. In a few short years he had made of an effervescent, hysterical people one of the grandest nations on earth, and given it a system of government nobler and more realist than the world has ever known. Mosley came back from Italy tremendously impressed with the Italian leader and the spiritually regenerated Italian people. More than ever did he perceive the necessity for applying the Fascist solution to modern problems. This is how he described Fascism in an article which he wrote immediately after his return:-

"It is as remote from a stand-pat Conservatism as it is from the woolly headed Socialism or the destructive Communism which it overthrew. It brings to post-war politics a new creed and a new philosophy which cannot be tucked away in any of the old pigeonholes of thought. On the one hand, that creed provides order, discipline, stability, authority, the 'play in the team or get out' attitude of the modern movement, the steady march of the young ranks of Fascism under determined leadership. All these things suggest what the old world calls the 'Right,' and would send the average English Socialist into a nightmare of hysteria which gibbered of 'dictatorship' and 'tyranny'. On the other hand, this new faith has just produced constructive works to give the unemployed a job instead of the dole; the removal of landlords who are inefficient and the cultivation of their land by the State; the Labour Charter, which affirms that no man has rights unless he works; the Corporative Law, which gives the State not only the power of compulsory arbitration in labour disputes binding on both sides, but also unlimited power of interference and compulsion in cases of inefficient or anti-social use of capital. It has produced the greatest child-welfare system, which annually takes hundreds of thousands to the mountains and to the sea; the Doppolavoro (after work) club system for all workers, which is one of the most spectacular achievements of the Fascist regime; the 'political atmosphere,' which is liable to remove an obstructive employer or capitalist, as well as the Communist agitator, for a 'health holiday' on certain salubrious islands known as the 'Confino'. All these things would send the old-fashioned English Conservative shivering for protection to the 'respectable' Socialism of Mr. Arthur Henderson. In fact, we are dealing with something new and not yet understood in this country. This Fascism challenges alike the 'Right' and the 'Left' of old-world politics. It has produced not only a new system of government, but also a new type of man, who differs from the politicians of the old world as men from another planet."

Mosley saw working in Italy a method which effectively controlled every phase of economic and social life on behalf of the overriding interests of the nation as a whole - a method which made impossible the sectional rampages of Financial Democracy and allowed an entire nation to plan for its own future in an atmosphere of earnest and united effort, from which all the old dog-fights and games of bluff had been expelled. He was convinced that a British form of Fascism could achieve even greater results than those of Italian Fascism, first, because our vast Imperial resources would enable us, in a much quicker time, to insulate our system against the attacks of international finance, and, second, because the team spirit, which is the essence of Fascism, has been historically more Anglo-Saxon, than a Latin quality. He went also to Germany, where the similar movement of National Socialism was emerging to transform a defeated and demoralised nation, with seven million unemployed, into a great, resurgent power, tackling its tremendous difficulties in a spirit of regained manhood and impelled to heights of collective achievement by the genius, sincerity, and heroic inspiration of Adolf Hitler.

Confirmed upon his course of action by all that he had seen abroad, Mosley made up his mind to lead a Fascist movement in Britain - a movement freely acknowledging its debt to Hitler and Mussolini, but, nevertheless, distinctively British in policy and method, concerned solely with the welfare and greatness of the British people. He was not blind to the appalling, monumental difficulties that such a movement would encounter in its bid for power. The British public knew nothing about the philosophy, constructive proposals or achievements of Fascism in other countries. Incessant propaganda had assured them that it was nothing more than a tyranny, dolloping out castor-oil to its opponents and existing solely for the personal aggrandisement of Signor Mussolini. Apologists for a lawless capitalism and an equally chaotic democratic system assured the British people, standing on the verge of ruin, how lucky they were to retain their precious liberty of Press and platform, in charming complement to the very agencies by which they were fooled and enslaved. All the poison of misrepresentation that had once been spread against Russia was now being spread against the creeds of Mussolini and Hitler, which were much more feared by the general interests than a Socialism that had been bought out of existence in Britain with blandishments and bribes of office and of power. The modern movement had been represented, not as a revolutionary force destroying the systems of economic exploitation and political humbug which were a feature of financial democracy in every part of the globe, but as the actual instrument of that exploitation and of that humbug. In other words, reactionary capitalism in Britain derided and sought to damage Fascism by alleging that it was the agent of capitalist reaction - a quaint distortion which, coming from such a source, should have aroused the suspicion of British workers, but which they swallowed whole.

The effect of all this misrepresentation was not left out of Mosley's reckoning. He knew that all the old parties - Tory, Liberal, and Socialist - would join in a conspiracy to defend the corrupt democratic system, and bring the might of their joint forces to bear against a really challenging Fascist movement in this country. He knew that every small incident during the revolutionary phases of Fascism in other countries would be collected and used as evidence against him. He knew that there already existed a legend that because he had abandoned one useless party after another he was no more than a quick-jumping turn-coat without stability or principle, and that his adoption of Fascism would not be regarded in true perspective, as an inevitable culmination of the evolutionary trend of his life's thought and experience, but as further confirmation of what was supposed to be his reckless opportunism and love of the limelight, no matter in what grotesque posture it caught him. He knew the force of this legend, as he knew the towering dimensions of the mass hatred of Fascism which had already been fostered against any such contingency, and which would reach gigantic proportions as soon as he began to make headway with his cause. He foresaw that all the violence of all the hooligan elements created during a hundred years of unscrupulous industrialism would be flung against him, and that all the political and financial elements would rejoice to see such a thing happening, and would, indeed, band themselves together to give it surreptitious support and even open vindication. He knew - the New Party experience had taught him - how colossal would be the effort needed to get his cause heard at all, let alone accepted, amidst the uproar and violence of uniformed multitudes taught to believe the absurdity that he came upon the scene as a monstrous tyrant to enslave them still further on behalf of the capitalists, whom they already had sufficient cause to loathe and fear. Mosley foresaw every one of these difficulties and he did not flinch. He had previously shown himself a man of immense courage. By launching his Fascist attack against the strongest conspiracy of vested powers in the world, he proved something more: he proved that his quality is as heroic as anything in the history of politics.

That the interests of the nation required (and more than ever require) the triumph of Fascist power and responsibility can be denied only by ignoring every single manifestation of its state and spirit. Slums and semi-slums everywhere. Malnutrition on a gigantic scale, while food is destroyed to keep up the profits of capitalism. Millions unemployed while the people cry aloud for the products of their labour. Usury and every other form of parasitism feeding upon the decay of a great people. Election promises made only to be broken, to serve the sordid little careers of political nincompoops. Distraction from the contemplation of internal grievances by a foreign policy interfering in the affairs of stronger and better governed nations, and alternately inviting disastrous wars and humiliating the British name by crawling away from them by the skin of Baldwin's teeth and the outer fringe of Eden's dashing moustache. Government too weary, too cowardly, and too incompetent to govern. Criminal neglect of defence. A mighty Empire sliding adrift where it is not actually given away. Absolute lack of any policy for an economic position which must gravely deteriorate as boom periods shorten and periods of depression lengthen in the final breakdown of capitalism. These are only a few of the symptoms indicating the nation's sickness, and they are not even the most serious symptoms.

Still more important is the degradation of all values to what are known in the theatre as box-office values. After the War a debased commercial civilisation reached the apotheosis in a riot of vulgarity and spoliation. Financial tyranny of the worst kind was exerted to force down and destroy all previous standards of commercial morality. The business ethic of giving value for money disappeared over the horizon into the limbo of lost decencies. Pride in the product gave way to the obsession of profit. Goods in hundreds of instances were specially constructed to break easily or soon wear out in order that there might be orders for replacement. The scandal of Local Government became steadily worse. The fair face of England wore the aspect of a progressive ugly rash of jerry-building, so that builders might make extra profits by scamping their jobs. The noble English theatre became the happy hunting ground of speculative vulgarians and Nancies degrading public taste to levels upon which they would find no difficulty in supplying the demand that they themselves created. The cinema - a cultural medium of the first importance - was captured by American and Polish Jew financiers and made to contribute to the general demoralisation of the people. It either neglected or befouled the English scene, so full of pageantry and memories of colourful adventure and daring, to superimpose a bastardised Judaic-American pseudo-culture upon a nation with a superb cultural inheritance of its own. The Press, with its extraordinary opportunities for high service to Britain, threw away that opportunity in order to exploit commercial values and political intrigues, making itself the disseminator of all that is sensational and vicious instead of all that is fine in the life of man, and spurning to give honest news and enlightening opinion, because more commercial and political profit can be extracted from the concealment, distortion, and downright betrayal of the truth. The ether became full of bad jazz and the heart throbs of a-sexual crooners Life took on the air of a kind of *palais de danse*. Art gave up the attempt to speak in praise of health, and suffered itself to become the vehicle of sickness and decay. Poetry no longer aspired to be the language of heroes, but the lisp of the spiritually diseased. Novelists refined emotions to the tenuity of a split hair, out-Freuding Freud. Biography set to work elevating the morale of an age of dwarfs by debunking all the heroes and great men of the past, leaving, for memory of them, only a series of nasty little smells. Everywhere else the worship of money or the exaltation of decay. C.E.M. Joad ran from "the cloven hoof of Fascism" to propose to the Oxford Union that under no circumstances should they fight for their King and Country, and the spiritually castrated young gentlemen agreed that they were much too exquisite to fight in defence of a country which gave them their undeserved advantages. Pacifism spread forth from these grand old centres of what had once been England's intellectual life to contaminate youth throughout the land and leave them unfit for the war with their exhibitionism and folly. The hard-faced men of Mosley's first Parliament and their hard-faced friends have extended their dominion to cover the whole of the nation's economic life. The nation's intellectual and artistic life has passed into the keeping of she-men and he-women. Spiritually the victory has gone to the conscientious objectors who betrayed the nation's dead. In a world of resurgent nations Britain - once so splendid and vital - is plundered and debased and vitiated, surrendering every claim to health and greatness and dynamic life.

Throughout the post-War period Mosley was aware of all these things and saw in them a ghastly mockery of every fair hope for Britain which had helped so many men die for her. But because Fascism undertakes responsibility for the spiritual health of the nation, no less than for the sane ordering of its economic and social life, he will not rest until this deplorable decadence of the mind and soul and body of Britain has been cut away in the surge and spirit of a race reborn.

14 - Olympia And The Jews

While Mosley was drawing up his plans the New Party movement kept his proposals before the public at meetings held in London and many provincial towns. To these proposals was now added another - that of the corporate structure of the State which is a distinctive feature of Fascist policy. It was represented by opponents as a notion that had come quite fortuitously into Mosley's head, whereas, in fact - and as we have seen - he put forward a plea for granting employees an equal partnership with the employers in the control of industry as long back as his Harrow days, when, in consequence, he had been described by a "Left" journal as a Guild Socialist. The corporate structure he now advocated was no other thing than the scientific method of giving effect to his old desire to secure a square deal for the workers, and was completely in line with one of the guiding principles of his political career.

During the first few months of 1932 negotiations were in progress for the launching of the Fascist movement in Britain. There were already in existence - unfortunately for Mosley in one sense, though not in another - several British Fascist movements. Unfortunately, because, for the most part, they had little knowledge of what Fascism meant apart from its patriotism, and had, therefore, lent themselves whenever needed to protect the meetings of the Conservative Party; seeking in vain, apparently, for any less dubious form of patriotic activity. They tended to confirm the suggestion which had been so assiduously fostered that Fascism was an extreme wing of Conservatism - a purely reactionary force. On the other hand, there were many excellent men and women in their ranks, and among them people who believed in real Fascism and were only too anxious to find a real leader.

The first and largest of these organisations from which most of the subsequent and smaller movements were formed was the "British Fascisti," founded on May 6, 1923, and incorporated as a limited company on May 7, 1924. The "British Fascists," as this movement was afterwards called, claimed to be a non-political, patriotic organisation. They were violently anti-Communist, and were formed mainly for the purpose of assisting the authorities in the event of a national emergency, which, at the time of its formation, seemed likely to arise. The organisation reached its peak during the General Strike of 1926, when its membership was estimated at half a million. Its failure to become an effective political force is to be attributed to lack of leadership and a definite Fascist policy.

The "National Fascisti" was formed early in 1925 by a few ex-members of the British Fascists. They adopted a black shirt and a more virile policy. After a comparatively short existence, they closed down, due to difference of opinion among their senior officers and also to the financial difficulties in which they found themselves. After a few weeks, a certain number of their members joined together and reformed the movement under the title, "British National Fascisti," which had a somewhat chequered career and ceased to function shortly after an article regarding it had appeared in "*John Bull.*"

The "British Empire Fascists," the "Fascist League," the "Imperial Fascist League," the "Empire Fascist Movement," and the "Fascist Movement" all had a brief existence during the years 1923 to 1932. It was with the British Fascists that the New Party established contact through N. Francis-Hawkins, one of the leaders of the former movement.

In February, 1932, at the request of Dr. Robert Forgan, he met Sir Oswald Mosley for the first time. Prior to this interview he had attended several meetings addressed by Mosley and had been much impressed. At the interview it was agreed that the aims of the two movements were very similar, and that it was foolish to carry on separate organisations and propaganda.

Francis-Hawkins therefore suggested that he should approach the Executive Council of the British Fascists, of which he was a member, and ascertain their views as to an amalgamation of the two movements.

After several weeks of unofficial discussion with officials of the New Party, he reported to the Executive of the British Fascists that he was in touch with the New Party and put forward the suggestion for an amalgamation. The Executive expressed interest in the proposal, and appointed him liaison officer to negotiate on their behalf with Sir Oswald Mosley for a union. At further meetings between the members of the Executive Council and Sir Oswald's representatives, a memorandum setting out a definite basis of organisation for the fusion was prepared and tentatively accepted by officials of the British Fascists, subject to confirmation at a full executive meeting. At this meeting, which was held in May, 1932, the three members of the council representing the women's units decided to oppose the scheme and recommended that further negotiations with the New Party be discontinued. The three male members of the council supported the scheme for a fusion, but as the council had a membership of six the meeting resulted in a deadlock.

Disgusted with the sudden change of the attitude of the council, Francis-Hawkins rendered his resignation from that body and also his membership of the British Fascists, and associated himself with Mosley in the formation of the new movement. The other two male members of the British Fascists' Council followed soon afterwards, and by October 1, the date on which the new movement came into existence, the entire effective strength of the British Fascists had accepted the leadership of Sir Oswald Mosley. Thus came to be formed the British Union of Fascists, with headquarters still at Great George Street.

The men who were still with Mosley had been, without exception, the only people whom he had been able to place in absolute reliance during the short, turbulent life of the New Party, and they were destined to do still finer work in the days ahead. Prominent among them were "Bill" Risden, now chief political agent, and R.A. Plathen, now chief organiser in Scotland - both splendid men. Among those joining Mosley from the British Fascists was, as we have seen, Francis-Hawkins, whose remarkable gifts of organisation have carried him through various subordinate posts to become the present Director-General of Organisation and a tower of strength to the cause. Other important recruits (now veterans) included men of outstanding ability such as Dundas, Piercy, Joyce, Beckett, Raven Thomson, and Finlay, all of whom have played a magnificent part in the building up of the Fascist movement. Ian Hope Dundas, as chief of staff, brings the traditions of the naval officer to the task of securing equity within the movement, in which he received every support from his deputy, A.G. Finlay. Eric Hamilton Piercy - forced to resign an inspectorship in the special constabulary because of his support for Mosley - organised and led the Fascist stewards through all the battles of the streets and halls that had to be fought before the Fascist case could be heard by British audiences. William Joyce, brilliant writer, speaker, and exponent of policy, has addressed hundreds of meetings, always at his best, always revealing the iron spirit of Fascism in his refusal to be intimidated by violent opposition. He is today the British Union's Director of Propaganda. John Beckett is the editor-in-chief of all Fascist publications, and he has also done invaluable work for the movement as a forceful writer and a speaker of great eloquence and power. He had a distinguished - if somewhat hectic - career as a Labour Member of Parliament until disillusionment came, and he refused to work longer with useless colleagues. Raven Thomson is an interesting example of the way in which Fascist inspiration transforms thoughtful types of men into men of action. A philosopher and critic of Spengler, Thomson has, nevertheless, gone out to face angry mobs in the streets and has shown the greatest pluck throughout his service. He has a remarkable gift for clear exposition and is the movement's Director of Policy.

The British Union of Fascists (now officially the British Union of Fascists and National Socialists, more briefly known as the British Union) began its career on October 3, 1933, when Mosley, in person, hoisted the Fascist banner outside the Great George Street premises. It was on this date, too, that his book, "The Greater Britain," made its first appearance - certainly one of the profoundest and most stimulating studies of post-war British politics to issue from the printing press. So well was it written and so incontrovertible its argument, that even the newspapers most expert at the game had the greatest difficulty in reviewing it with derision.

Now, for the first time, Mosley's supporters appeared wearing the black shirt, which they were so soon to make famous. Mosley's arguments in favour of a political uniform carry conviction. He affirms that men dedicated to a cause, and serving it with religious fervour, have a natural desire to express symbolically their deep, inner feelings, and that the more dynamic that cause, the more intense the loyalties which it arouses, the bolder will be the symbols chosen. Moreover, Fascists fighting for the soul of Britain in times of peace are no less enlisted on behalf of their country's service than soldiers fighting for its security in times of war, and are, therefore, proud to wear no less unequivocal a uniform. There is, as well, the strictly utilitarian reason that when meetings are attacked by mobs of alien thugs and Red razor-slashers, it is undeniably useful as a means of enabling the Blackshirts, sometimes outnumbered by hundreds to one, to act together as a disciplined body. It serves admirably, too, in eliminating distinctions of dress as between the well-to-do and the poor in a movement which seeks to break down all barriers of class. Finally, the black shirt requires courage to wear, and that with Mosley is a powerful argument in its favour, since his cause has suffered a good deal in the past from chicken-hearted democrats who proved themselves unreliable in times of danger. Mosley saw that the new movement would have to advance with iron determination towards its objectives, and its inner core of devoted followers would need more than the usual amount of pluck. It was, therefore, expedient to have so simple a test at the outset of a recruit's service. Not that the wearing of the black shirt is obligatory upon the general membership. At the present time business and other considerations allow only one member in every twenty to wear the uniform, so vicious has been the campaign of victimisation conducted by employers and others against men and women suspected of Fascist sympathies. The decision was typical of Mosley's bold leadership. He had been assured that political uniform would be anathema to the British people, and when he and his few early followers first donned the black shirt there was no guarantee that a single soul would follow suit. It so happens, however, that the move has more than justified itself, and today tens of thousands of young Britons wear the uniform with resolution and pride.

Another very wise step taken by Mosley was to shut out the self-seekers by insisting at the start that service should entail sacrifice. The movement has never possessed the fabulous resources attributed to it, and every available penny has gone, not to secure highly paid staff-officers, but to organise along Spartan lines for victory. Its rapid growth has demanded an increasing number of full-time officials, but in every instance they have accepted the smallest possible remuneration for their living expenses and regarded the balance of payment as being simply restored by the privilege to serve. This fine spirit has done British Fascism the inestimable service of keeping away the democratic gold-digging mentality which would have tried to use the movement for purposes of personal gain.

Since that day in October when Mosley unfurled the first Fascist banner his movement has flourished beyond expectation. Several factors have contributed to its success, not the least of them being Mosley's power of great leadership, which was more than ever revealed when Fascist organisation succeeded the semi-democratic organisation of the New Party. Gone were the half-hearted colleagues who wished to debate every trifling issue for days before arriving at a decision. Gone were the pompous local committees "refusing to play" whenever decisions were not acceptable to them. In place of talk there was now action; and in place of the local committee there was now the resolute executive officer, enormously keen, undertaking full responsibility for his branch and either carrying out orders with alacrity or making way for a better man. It has sometimes happened that when branch officers have "fallen down" on their jobs and been replaced, other members of the branch have banded together in sympathy with him to make representations to Headquarters, in the meantime seeking to bring pressure to bear by withholding co-operation. Their surprise has been intense on finding themselves cleared out "neck and crop" in every instance, even when it has meant closing down an active branch. By these methods Mosley has safeguarded British Fascism from the corrupting influences which undermine all democratic parties and lead to their eternal substitution of compromise for leadership and action. On matters of principle Mosley never has and never will compromise, and the British Union is built on the rock of that determination.

Another direction in which Mosley has sped forward the growth of Fascism is his absolute refusal to submit to intimidation by Red mobs inflamed against him by the old party leaders and the old party Press. From the outset, these mobs, often subsidised, have endeavoured to drive the Blackshirt off the streets by methods of extreme violence. At the British Union's first meeting in Trafalgar Square the Blackshirts were obliged to defend themselves against attack and at almost every meeting that followed during the next few months organised hooliganism threatened to smash up the proceedings. To meet this menace the Blackshirts evolved a very efficient technique of ejecting unruly elements from halls and of protecting their speakers on the street corners. This side of their work has been perhaps the most inspiring thing to witness since the war. Night after night for weeks and months and years the devoted young Blackshirts have given up their ease, spurned the cinema and the dance hall and all other recreations in order to defend Blackshirt speakers from the arguments of cosh and razor and broken bottles. At weekends they have accompanied their Leader or senior Fascist speakers to break new ground in distant industrial towns, and no call has ever been made on them to which they have failed to respond. As a result of their self-sacrifice and their refusal to be disheartened by many a brick and chair on the head or razor slash on the face, they have commanded a hearing for the Fascist case, and that, in turn, has enabled British audiences to learn at first hand the creed of the British Blackshirt movement. In a large number of districts which were once Red strongholds - notably in the East End of London - where not long ago frenzied attacks on Fascists were the rule rather than the exception, there are today mass Fascist movements loyal to the cause and hailing Mosley as the liberator of Britain.

Before these victories were achieved, however, there were some terrific battles in halls and streets all over the country - in Manchester, Newcastle, Bristol, and, in fact, wherever thugs in sufficient numbers could be pressed into service against the Fascist march to power. At Kentish Town, in London, a handful of stewards found hundreds of angry toughs crammed into the hall when Mosley spoke. They greeted him with howls and catcalls, drowning every word he uttered, but the young stewards, outnumbered by about thirty to one, sprang into the arena and started to eject them in shoals amidst fierce fighting in which many of them were seriously injured. Piercy and Plathen were taken to hospital with heads bleeding profusely, only to return, bandaged, to help in the restoration of order. So magnificent an account of themselves did the Blackshirts give that at another meeting held in the same hall a few months later Joyce was able to speak with scarcely an interruption. And so has it been almost everywhere else. Inspired by Mosley's own indomitable courage and by the courage of his lieutenants, the young Blackshirts have taught even the ugliest Red gangs to respect the Fascist name, and never to attack unless their numbers are at least twenty to one.

While there seemed a likelihood of these battles ending in victory for the Reds, the old gang politicians of both Right and Left were well content not to intervene, but the moment it became clear that the disciplined force of British Fascism was overcoming the rabble, and allowing the one man in Britain whom they really feared to address great and increasingly enthusiastic audiences, they sent up a series of cries about "Blackshirt brutality" and "Blackshirt provocation," even though there was no single instance of a Blackshirt charged with disturbances at an opposition meeting, while scores of Reds had been convicted for violence at Fascist demonstrations, even though the Blackshirts, always heavily outnumbered, were manifestly concerned only to protect their own meetings; and even though many Conservative members had experienced, and usually succumbed to, the same kind of Red ruffianism. Noting the remarkable success of the Blackshirts they shrieked out that it was this factor which inflamed the good, honest, patriotic Red mobs against Fascism. Beckett very courageously volunteered to demonstrate the absurdity of this parrot-cry by speaking without the usual Blackshirt stewards at a huge gathering at Newcastle. Directly the speech began about a thousand roughs in front set up a roar in which nothing could be heard, and a rush was then made for the platform. Only the fortunate fact that Piercy, Risdon, and three other headquarters officers, all in plain clothes, happened to be in the crowd watching the experiment, prevented Beckett from receiving terrible injuries. They came charging to his assistance and held the mob at bay until the police belatedly intervened. What happened then was described by the Blackshirt in these words:-

"This action on the part of the police, who had been reinforced by an inspector who had watched the attempts to assault Mr. Beckett with great interest, emboldened the crowd to make a further rush. The Fascists, who were then ten in number, again drove the crowd back, and the police were willing to accept shelter behind them without further interference. The little group with their backs to the monument were now assailed with broken bottles, heavy stones, and every kind of missile, two of them being badly knocked about. Two mounted police then arrived, and although they made no effort to check or control the crowd, their presence enabled our men to start back for headquarters. The mounted police and four policemen on foot accompanied them, keeping out of the way of the stream of projectiles thrown by the crowds who ran on each side. Entering the headquarters, one member was stunned by a heavy brick and two other members were injured. Every hooligan in Newcastle had by now been concentrated outside headquarters. For two hours this crowd waited outside, and three members attempting to leave the building were knocked out before they had crossed the street. A young member in plain clothes who had been visiting the club with a lady, left the building. They were both attacked by a large crowd. The young woman was knocked down. This was too much for our men, and about twenty Blackshirts with the visitors from London made a sally. There were small groups of our men defending themselves in different parts of the street. One who had been looking after an elderly man who had been hurt and had been set upon by about thirty men, was arrested by the police. He had inadvertently struck a plain clothes policeman who came at him with the rest. Another, who had been cut off by the crowd, was arrested for the same offence. While the police, now in considerable strength, marched Davis to the station, they raised no objection to rowdies kicking him all the way, and one well known local Communist leader stopped the procession, struck him, and walked away. These were the only two arrests made by the police. In the melee the Communists used every kind of iron bar and leaded club, jagged broken bottles, huge lumps of brick, a boy scout's knife with both blades open, and parcels of brown paper containing heavy stones. Ten of our men were treated for serious injuries. The City Police now suggest that Blackshirts should abandon their meetings in Newcastle."

I quote this passage in full to give some idea of the ordeals to which Fascists have been exposed in Britain and also to demonstrate, the dishonesty of those who seek to ascribe Red violence to the wearing of the black shirt. It is only fair to the police to state that elsewhere they have performed their duties with strict impartiality.

Old-gang support of mob-style rule against Fascism reached its height over the huge Olympia meeting held by Mosley in 1934. Perhaps the mightiest indoor rally ever held in Britain, Mosley had no sooner begun to speak than it became clear that organised Red gangs, each hundreds strong, were occupying strategic positions in every part of the huge arena - even in the most expensive seats - with the sole intention of preventing the speech being heard. Five or six in one part of the hall would create a din, and when Blackshirt stewards approached to eject them scores of Red colleagues would arise to join in the battle. There would be a fierce struggle, resulting in the Reds being bundled out of the building, whereupon the same tactics would be employed in another part of the building. So it went on for two long hours, during which the thousands present learnt nothing about Fascism except the bravery and pertinacity of its young adherents in dealing with a very perilous situation. Finally, however, the last gang was flung out of the hall and Mosley was able to speak without interruption for the remaining hour and to bring the meeting to an end amidst scenes of the greatest enthusiasm.

The sequel was heard in Parliament. Member after member rose to take the part of the Red rabble and to condemn in the most sweeping and grotesque fashion the action of British manhood in defending their mighty rally from being wrecked by the mob. Lie after lie was told in order to try to besmirch the Blackshirt name. The stewards were virtually accused of turning a peaceful meeting into a riot by utterly unprovoked attacks on respectable, law abiding citizens. Although the Blackshirts met knives, coshes, broken bottles, and all other weapons of the Ghetto with only their bare fists they themselves were charged by dishonest Parliamentarians with using these instruments. It was one of the most disgraceful episodes in the history of the House of Commons, this defamation of brave men, but aimed as it was at Mosley it redounded to his advantage in that the huge audience, who had seen what actually occurred, had an admirable opportunity of judging the veracity of the Members of Parliament who lent their voices to the cause of the Red ape-men whom the Blackshirts had managed to bundle out of the premises so that Mosley might be heard.

I have said "weapons of the Ghetto," because at this and every other rowdy Fascist meeting the Jews have taken the lead in stirring up disorder. Funds for the buying of tickets for rowdies at Olympia, for example, were traced in many instances to Jewish sources, and many Jewish faces were also to be seen among the mob. This may be a suitable place, therefore, to give a summary of Mosley's views on the Jewish question. At the beginning of his Fascist campaign these views were not very definite one way or the other. While it is probable that he had no deeper an affection for Jews in the mass than any other Englishman, the last thought in his head was that it would prove necessary for him to adopt any attitude towards them, apart from refusing them admittance to the movement - a step made essential by the power of the Jew in an incredibly short time to gain control for himself and his fellow-racials of organisations with which he became associated. Even today Mosley refuses to be drawn into adopting any racial line of attack on them, holding that an Empire composed of many different races, castes, colours, and creeds precludes any possibility of racial persecution, even if persecution were held to be otherwise desirable, which he denies. When questioned about his attitude towards Jews, his reply has always been along these lines: "Fascism has declared war on every kind of anti-social activity, from the jugglings of international finance down to the organisation of vice trades in great cities; in so far as the Jew is identified with any of these activities, so far but no further need he fear the Fascist advent to power. The Jew who conducts himself as a decent citizen, obeying the laws of the Corporate State, paying in accordance with the high wage system required of every employer, conforming to price-regulations, and putting the interests of Britain above those of international Jewry, will not be in any way molested. Jews who refuse to observe these requirements will be treated exactly as other enemies of the people will be treated, absolutely without racial discrimination." That was Mosley's position at the beginning, and it is still his position, even though in the meantime he has accepted the challenge which Jews in their ignorance and folly have flung at the advance of British Fascism.

Mosley's attention was soon drawn to the fact that Jewish money was being poured into anti-Fascist activities; that the Jews were forming organisations which carted toughs around in vans to create uproar at Fascist meetings; that the influence of Jewry was making itself felt through all the media of "national" propaganda; and that no less than fifty percent of persons convicted of assaults on Fascists bore Jewish names. This puzzled him, until he caused an investigation to be made into Jewish financial and commercial activities in this country. Then he discovered the reason. He found that there is no great financial, industrial, or commercial trust or combine which was not dominated by the Jew, whether acting in person or by proxy. The whole capitalist racket, the whole of the national Press, the whole of the "British" cinema, and the whole bunch of purely parasitical occupations were found to be Jew-ridden. Every vitiating and demoralising factor in our national life was Jew-influenced where it was not Jew-controlled. Mosley thereupon took up the challenge, and as a result of the Jew daring to come between a great British leader and the great British people Fascism has gained more than it has lost, while the Jew has lost both on the roundabouts and the swings. Mosley, in a recent speech, underlined this fact at one of his tremendous rallies. After describing the opening rounds of the conflict with the Jews, he went on to declare: "Eighteen months ago this struggle was launched in Britain. All shrank from us. The great and powerful were afraid when our Fascist movement opened its crusade against Jewry. What has been the result? Our downfall was freely prophesied. When we began that struggle, when the Press deserted us, when the big guns ceased to fire, when we launched our challenge to Jewry, we possessed one hundred and sixty branches in Britain. Today we possess five hundred. And what of the force that was to break us? Are they stronger or weaker today? Up to three years ago anti-Semitism was unknown as a strong force in Great Britain. Today, in any audience in Britain, the strongest passion that can be aroused is the passion against the corruption of Jewish power. It is not we who perish in this struggle. We have fought because we were challenged and Britain was threatened; but the Jew himself has created anti-Semitism - created it as he has always done, by letting people see him and his methods. Even Hitler was not anti-Semitic before he saw a Jew. It was when they came out into the open, when they marched to Hyde Park and tried to drag us to war with Germany, when fear made them less cunning, when they revealed themselves to the British people. That was when anti-Semitism was born. When they dared to challenge Fascism for the first time in their lives they found a force, a power, and a spirit in Britain which money could not buy. And now we go on. We march forward to a victory which is inevitable, not by small illegalities or petty violence unworthy of a great movement, but with a great appeal to the whole of the British people, by disciplined methods characteristic of a mighty nation, to give to Fascism power by verdict of an electorate which knows we shall use that power in the British way to challenge and to break forever in Britain the power of the Jew."

15 - Persecution Unlimited

Mosley's reference to the "big guns" in his speech about the Jews concerned the Rothermere Press, which surprised every Fascist in the country by appearing in 1934 as a supporter of the Blackshirts. This would have been a powerful aid to the movement's progress, since Lord Rothermere is a great patriot, had it not been for his quaint misunderstanding as to the nature of Fascism. He published a picture of strike-breakers, for example, and gave it the legend: "This is the spirit of the Blackshirts." He imagined, it seems, that Mosley was a Right-Wing Tory, instead of a Fascist revolutionary, and that his movement existed to bolster up big business in Britain. Incalculable harm was done by this intervention, and the large influx of recruits which resulted proved useless to a man. There was a sigh of relief when his Lordship repented in haste and celebrated his dropping of the Blackshirts with two leading articles full of ludicrous praise of the Jews - a matter of no small significance. No doubt, had Mosley been willing to toe the line to Rothermere and abandon most of the principles that he held dear, the "big guns" would today still be booming on his side. But Mosley is not made of that kind of stuff.

The movement prospered far better on its own, without such half-hearted and embarrassing support. Mosley's innumerable great rallies in different parts of Britain recruited far finer types of men and women than would be likely to respond to the call of any Press lord. As "Red" violence has been progressively overcome, and mass Fascist movements have taken its place in district after district, so has it become possible for the Leader and his chief speakers to address scores of thousands of people in parks and open spaces. In Victoria Park recently the police estimated the audience at 100,000, ninety percent of whom gave Mosley one of the most enthusiastic receptions of his life. There have also been the marvellous Albert Hall demonstrations, with their arrays of banners, their fanfares, their triumphal entries of the Leader, their singing of Fascist songs, their acclamation of Mosley's inspired oratory, and all their other evidence proclaiming that at last the men and women of Britain have found a cause to love and a leader to follow to the death. The extraordinary success of these meetings, both indoor and outdoor, have thrown the democratic politicians into a state bordering on hysteria, and the House of Commons is constantly resounding with the noise of their panic. So irresistible is Mosley's propaganda that his opponents are going to almost any length in their efforts to stop it. As soon as a hall is booked for any Fascist meeting opponents get busy locally presenting petitions and sending deputations to induce the authorities to cancel the letting. Town Councils often refuse the hiring of town halls. The Labour majority on the L.C.C., thoroughly alarmed, are endeavouring to prevent the use of loudspeakers by Fascists at their demonstrations in the London parks. At Hulme, in Manchester, the Reds attack the Blackshirt headquarters and smash all the windows, whereupon the Manchester Watch Committee sends a deputation to the Home Office to protest, not against Red violence, but against the wearing of uniform by Fascists, on the specious plea that it is the uniform which causes all the trouble. Everywhere there is the same persecution as Mosley goes from triumph to triumph in spite of all the obstacles put in his way, in spite of all the violence, in spite of all the squealing, in spite of what is now virtually a united front of all the old gangs against him. The old parties forget their own political creeds in order to oppose his march. Conservatives, Liberals, and Socialists huddle together in a last futile effort to stave off the inevitable victory of a resurgent British manhood come at last to cleanse the temple of their native land in a fashion very different from that of Lloyd George, who first used the phrase.

Among the more serious persecutions which Mosley has had to face was a truly remarkable indictment for riotous assembly - a charge of great gravity. It followed an incident at Worthing, where an entirely satisfactory and peaceful meeting was held inside the Pier Pavilion. A crowd had gathered outside, and among them were some notorious anti-Fascists from other parts of the country, who had come, as was usual, solely for the purpose of creating a row. The meeting over, Mosley led his men outside and the mob immediately surged forward to attack him. As it is not the Mosley tradition when assaulted to throw up hands and cry "Kamerad," the Fascist leader proceeded to defend himself, and his Blackshirt followers gave him a hand. The incident, being one of many, was speedily forgotten by Mosley, when to his surprise, ten days later, he and three of his officers (including Joyce) were summoned to answer a charge of riotous assembly. The case dragged on for days at the Worthing Police Court, and Mosley, under cross-examination by Mr. John Flowers, K.C., counsel for the prosecution, had the opportunity of stating exactly what he thought about the case and trumped-up evidence brought against him. The following dialogue comes as near as possible to describing his thoughts:

Counsel: Do you suggest that this prosecution is an afterthought?

Mosley: I should put it higher than that.

Counsel: Whose afterthought do you suggest?

Mosley: Far be it from me to know.

Counsel: Do you suggest it is an afterthought of the police?

Mosley: I would suggest that it is an afterthought of the authorities behind the police.

Counsel: Who are you suggesting are the authorities behind the police?

Mosley: The police, as I understand it, are controlled by the Government of the day; are they not?

Counsel: Are you seriously suggesting that this prosecution has been brought by the Government of the day?

Mosley: I believe it has been brought about by political considerations.

Counsel: I want to be quite clear as to your meaning. I suppose you mean by that that some political party has influenced the police of West Sussex to institute this prosecution. Is that what you mean?

Mosley: I suggest that, yes. I can give no other explanation for the bringing of this case.

Counsel: Are you suggesting that the individual members of the Worthing Police have given false evidence against you?

Mosley: That was my impression, yes.

Counsel: Are you suggesting that?

Mosley: I certainly think their evidence was contradictory and false.

Throughout the case Mosley defended himself with sparkling ability and wit. Superintendent Bristowe, in charge of the police, had given evidence that the mob were all "very nice people." Mosley's derisive comment in the box was: "I do not think the song they were singing, 'We want Mosley, dead or alive,' is a song that is universally known among nice people." Another passage-at-arms with the prosecuting counsel showed Mosley's refusal to be intimidated:

Counsel: Did you make any complaint to any policeman at all?

Mosley: It is not my habit to complain.

Counsel: The answer, then, is "No."

Mosley: The answer is "No" in my own way, and I do not require any instructions from you on how to give my evidence. If there is any necessity to correct me their Worships will do it. To be offensive is not the monopoly of King's Counsel, and the sooner you learn it the better.

Another deft reply, in lighter vein, was his answer to counsel's question: "The whole idea of your organisation on the streets is to hang together, is it not?"

"I trust not to hang together," said Mosley, amidst laughter.

A little later he stated that in a High Court case he had been believed after a cross-examination lasting the whole day long on credibility.

Counsel: Do be accurate: It was only four hours.

Mosley: Three and a half to be precise, and that is the greater part of a legal day, is it not?

Mosley's evidence was supported by a host of witnesses, including several women spectators, who described the violence and obscenity of the mob, but that did not prevent the old gentlemen of the Worthing Bench from committing the defendants for trial. When the case came before the Lewes Assizes it was derisively dismissed without the defence being called upon to answer the charge. Whatever the intention lay behind the prosecution, it was frustrated by British justice, which today, in its higher reaches at least, is one of the few honest institutions left to the British people.

The remark made by Mosley about a High Court case referred to an action for libel which he brought against the Daily News

Ltd., proprietors of *The Star* newspaper. It arose out of a public debate which he had with James Maxton, in which he stressed the fact that in the event of a Red insurrection in this country, Fascism would be ready to meet the Communists if need be, with machine-guns, since Fascists are unalterably loyal to the Throne. This was distorted by *The Star* to suggest something altogether different. Their exact words were: "Sir Oswald Mosley warned Mr. Maxton that he and his Fascists would be ready to take over government with machine-guns when the time arrived. Mr. Tom Mann was recently thrown into prison on the mere suspicion that he might say something ten times less provocative than Sir Oswald Mosley's words." Addressing the jury on Mosley's behalf, Sir Patrick Hastings asked: "Now, members of the jury, what can those words mean? They can only mean one thing, in my submission, that Sir Oswald Mosley has stated that he was prepared to take over government by force, which can mean nothing else than a traitorous, rebellious act, and secondly, that what he said was so bad that it was ten times worse than the words of a man who had already been thrown in prison for using them quite lately. In this country a man is not thrown into prison unless he has been guilty of a criminal offence, and if a man has been thrown into prison by law, and Sir Oswald Mosley is a man who has said something ten times worse, can it mean anything else but that Sir Oswald Mosley is a man who ought to be thrown into prison under the law?"

The course taken by the defendant company was amazing. It said that the words were true, but presented no single witness to affirm their truth. It pleaded justification, but made no attempt to justify its statements to court. Instead, it added insult to injury by instructing counsel to cross-examine Mosley as to credibility - that is, to establish a case that he was not a person whose word could be accepted. Mr. Norman Birkett, K.C., met his match when he came to carry out his instructions, because Mosley emerged from a gruelling three hours as satisfactorily as it is possible for any man to do. The cross-examination became a debate of almost unparalleled keenness, which I should like to set down verbatim, but since this is impossible, I give only the following passage:-

Counsel: In that crisis which we discussed this morning, the Communist rising when you take machine-guns: is it in that crisis that you impose the Corporate State?

Mosley: You cannot, obviously, impose any rational system during a period of crisis. The Corporate State is not like a ready-made suit of clothes. It is something which you can introduce when you are in power, owing to the votes of the people.

Counsel: Suppose a Communist Government was in power with the assent of the King?

Mosley: A Communist Government?

Counsel: Yes: would you face them still with guns?

Mosley: That is a hypothetical question on a wild hypothesis that I have never seen.

Counsel: If a Communist Government is called to power with the assent of the King, would you shoot them down?

Mosley: It is possible to put a question on ever-increasing hypothesis which lead at last to an absurdity. You might as well say that if His Majesty the King of England enacted the law of Herod that every first-born shall be slain, would you, in those circumstances, be a revolutionary? The question you have put is a hypothetical absurdity.

Counsel: Can you answer it?

Mosley: You cannot answer questions which are by their very

nature absurd.

Counsel: Are you going to shoot the Old Gang, by any chance?

Mosley: What a very foolish and unnecessary thing for anybody to do!

Counsel: It is now conceded that the Fascist movement in this country is organised in two ways, one to capture power in normality, as you term it, in the ordinary way, public meetings, voting, and so on; secondly, it is an organisation to meet force in the State by force. Is that right?

Mosley: When it is used against the State.

Counsel: Who is to be the judge - you?

Mosley: When there is a condition of anarchy it does not require much judgement. If you were shot in the streets it would not require any great condition of judgement to know that you had been shot.

Counsel: Let me put this, and press it. Who are you to interfere with the forces of law and order which are in the country to maintain order against all revolution?

Mosley: Good heavens, no. I never suggested interfering with the forces of law and order. You will find in this book ("The Greater Britain"), from which you have been quoting extensively, a phrase to the effect that under no circumstances should we ever use force against forces of the Crown.

Counsel: It is the first time in this country, is it not, in our peaceful evolution of late years that a political leader has used language saying, "I am going to judge the moment when I use guns in the street"?

Mosley: No. Lord Carson said hundreds of things far worse
          than that at a time when he was a leader at the Bar.

Counsel: It is the first time in this country, is it not, in the
          government of our own country that any leader has
          said, "I will judge when the guns will shoot"?

Mosley: When did I say I should be the judge?

Counsel: Well, who is?

Mosley: It does not require much judgement. If I saw a
          policeman knocked down with two toughs stamping
          on him, it does not require the exercise of judgement
          to know whether one ought to intervene or not.

The cross-examination gave Mosley the opportunity of exposing
several other Press lies about his movement, notably those
dealing with armoured cars and aeroplanes. Because some young
enthusiasts in Gloucester learnt to fly a Moth plane Mosley was
accused of starting a Fascist Air Force: because his stewards were
transported to and from meetings in brick-proof vans he was
declared by the newspapers to have invested in armoured cars. Sir
Patrick Hastings, who appeared for Mosley, opened a devastating
fire on *The Star's* conduct throughout the case. "Members of the
jury," he said, "you may not appreciate what cross-examination
to credit and credibility means, but I am going to tell you. It
means this: if a witness comes into the witness-box to give
evidence, you may cross-examine him as to the facts of the case,
you may cross-examine him as to things which are material and
relevant, or you may say, 'I am going to challenge your veracity
and honesty,' and, if so, you may cross-examine him practically
upon any ground with the view of asking the jury to say that the
witness is not speaking the truth. Of course, speaking the truth is
a very, very mild phrase to use to a man who is giving evidence in

the witness-box. Sir Oswald Mosley was cross-examined to his credit, and on no less than three occasions Mr. Birkett stated that it was, of course, upon the instructions of *The Star* that cross-examination was directed to Sir Oswald Mosley. It could not have been done otherwise. Do you realise what this means? Until this moment Sir Oswald, I imagine, has always thought he had borne an honest name and was an honest man, just like any other person in the public eye. The leader of any of the other parties might bring an action against a newspaper of opposing political views. It certainly seemed a dreadful thing that a newspaper such as this should have instructed their Counsel in open Court to state that they were going to cross-examine Sir Oswald Mosley to his credit, and the whole of the cross-examination is directed to that. Members of the jury, it is not unusual when you cross-examine a man for hours to his credit to refer in some degree in the final observations that you make to the effect of that cross-examination, but it has not even been referred to...... One does not know what is actuating the motives of *The Star*. They are a political newspaper, and they may say: 'Well, we are going to do anything that we can to injure some political party or person of who we do not approve.'"

Lord Chief Justice Hewart, before whom the case was heard, had even more severe remarks to make in his summing up, from which I select for quotation the following:- "You have heard the plaintiff's evidence. Did you, or did you not, believe him? Whatever you may think of his answer, did he or did he not appear to you to be a public man of no little courage, no little candour and no little ability? He was cross-examined for a long, long time. Did anything come of it?..... The problem does not seem to be a difficult one, and you may think that Sir Patrick Hastings was quite right when he says that in intent and in fact this is an undefended case...... Another matter is the fact that there is upon the record, and there remains upon the record, a plea that these words are true. A third matter is this; You know libel may be written in a letter to an individual. It is published if it is communicated to any third person. It may be written upon a postcard, but it may by the terrible power of the modern printing press be multiplied a thousand-fold and a hundred thousand-fold and distributed no one knows where and last nobody knows how long. We hear of the power of the Press. Somebody once said the real power of the Press is the power of suppression. The power of the Press is a great and wonderful thing, but if it can be misused what a terrible instrument it can be. When, one wonders, will all the copies of this issue of this newspaper have ceased to exist, and when will the impression created by these words have ceased to have any effect upon a man's mind. All those matters are matters which you may properly take into account, and, remember, this newspaper is not produced for fun. It is produced for profit, and if in the course of making profit by producing a newspaper those who are responsible defame a man by stigmatising him as a criminal then a jury may think it right to mark their sense of what has been done by making those who are responsible for that paper smart, and smart in the place where, at any rate, they are likely to be sensitive, and that is their pockets. If you find for the plaintiff here you are entitled - it is a matter entirely for your good judgement and good sense - to award him such a sum as will not merely compensate him for the injury which then you will have found to have been done to him, but such sum as will mark your sense of that which they have done."

The verdict was for £5,000 damages, in addition to costs, for Mosley. It is amusing, in view of the jury's finding and the tribute paid by the Lord Chief Justice, to note that some months later, on a subject no less grave (it was a libel based on a document proved to be a forgery and produced by an expelled member) Mosley was awarded only a farthing damages. "The luck of the Law Courts," he said with a smile and a shrug of the shoulders.

By this time the movement had long outgrown the premises of Great George Street and moved to the big building in King's Road, Chelsea, known to Blackshirts as "The Black House," and to the anti-Blackshirts as the "Fascist Fort" or the "Fascist

Barracks." Even the accommodation of this great edifice proved inadequate as its corridors began to resound with the tramp of new members enrolling by the thousand and as department after department was formed to cope with the gigantic organisation necessitated by the movement's rapid growth. The Black House served Fascism well for many months. It was the centre of its gay, bustling, and in a sense turbulent life - the intellectual and social as well as the organisational centre. Its offices were occupied by men working fourteen and fifteen hours a day: its lecture halls were the scene of Joyce's brilliant policy lessons, filled with students eager to learn everything about this new exciting crusade; its club-rooms rang with the laughter and songs of men who felt that the advent of Fascism had made life again worth living. When the movement became big enough, however, the Leader decided that decentralisation was essential in order that Fascism should take root as a living force in the various London districts, and at the right moment he surrendered the lease of the Chelsea building and ordered the removal of Headquarters to Sanctuary Buildings, Westminster, where they are at the present time, run entirely on business lines. This move has enormously stimulated the local growth of Fascism in London, since members make for their own district offices instead of spending time crossing the metropolis to offer services more usefully employed in their own areas. There is also a Northern Headquarters at Manchester, visited by the Leader and the Director-General of Organisation at least once a week, and a Scottish Headquarters at Edinburgh.

Great marches and rallies are being held throughout Britain. Membership increases at a faster rate than any other movement has known. The Fascist Press flourishes. Almost every week *Action* and *The Blackshirt*, under John Beckett, obtain a higher circulation. The *Fascist Quarterly*, under J.A. Macnab, gains in power. There is everywhere a sense of the inevitability of Fascist triumph.

It is not surprising to find, therefore, a corresponding increase in the violence of Red opponents. In July of 1936 the Leader faced a barrage of stones at Hull flung by a demented rabble, and a shot was fired at his car. On the same occasion he was leading a march when a small body of his followers was cut off and savagely kicked and beaten with iron bars and scythes. Mosley led the dash to their rescue and unquestionably saved them from terrible injuries. As it was, eighteen Blackshirts were badly hurt. So it goes on. The Press and Parliament, seriously alarmed at the sweeping advance of Fascism, expend their energies supporting the Red gangs and using every kind of dishonest method to discredit Mosley and his followers. But in vain.

During the whole of the time Mosley has suffered only one disaster, but that was irreparable. Early in 1933 his wife died, leaving two sons and a daughter. A heroic figure, a fine, generous spirit, a woman of high intelligence and the greatest charm, Lady Cynthia will always be honoured, not only for her own sake, but for her splendid work as a pioneer of Fascism in Britain. Her spirit marches on.

Otherwise the records tell only of obstacles overcome, of violence tamed, of irresistible advance. Speaking at the last Albert Hall rally, Mosley summed up the position in great language: "We have created from nothing in the space of little over three years a nationwide movement...... a movement which began in one small room with a handful of men, without money, without resources of any kind, and now possesses some five hundred branches. That has been done in the face of every effort of politicians of Parliament, of Press, of money, of corruption, and of all the material forces of this world. It has been done by one thing, and one thing alone, the spirit and the faith within the Blackshirt movement. That force which in so short a space of time has created a mighty thing is capable not only of saving the land we love, not only of redeeming this country from corruption, but is capable of giving to distracted Europe the leadership which it lacks today, and rallying the forces of mankind to a higher form of civilisation than the world has yet known."

16 - Fascist Economics

Fascism - or National Socialism - is a creed of universal validity, but of purely national application. Every nation, in other words, interprets and adopts its principles in accordance with the temperament of its own people and the specific problems which confront them, and in this and the next two chapters it is proposed to convey to the reader as briefly as possible what Mosley means when he speaks of Fascism in Britain. I will deal first with the economic aspects of his programme.

This country's relative prosperity was built up during the last century upon its export trade. British industry was the first to profit by the use of machinery in the exploitation of the markets of the world. The result was the establishment of a large commerce with other nations, who sent us raw materials in return for the manufactured goods which were exported to them in increasing volume. Our captains of industry, rubbing their hands at the handsome rewards reaped from their enterprise, were confident that the process would go on forever. So were the politicians and political scientists and philosophers who encouraged them to believe that they were the chosen favourites of fortune. Britain had become the workshop of the world, and it was incredible to our grandfathers that it should ever cease to occupy that favoured place. Their self-esteem was monumental. So long as British skill was available to produce manufactured goods for other nations, it was considered out of the question that foreigners should ever desire to manufacture their own goods. Therefore the entire stress of the nineteenth and twentieth centuries was placed on export trade. The moneyed class became very rich as a result of this world commerce, and there also came into existence a large, affluent, and contented middle-class. That was one consequence of the Industrial Revolution, and it was the only consequence that was held to matter. The other consequence received scant attention - that millions of British people were compelled to sell their labour at the lowest possible rates, and thus live poverty-stricken lives in black urban growths, known as industrial towns, which came to sprawl like a disease over the once fair face of Britain, denying sun and air and health to generations after generations doomed to inhabit them.

The reason for this betrayal of human values is not difficult to find. So busy were the industrialists meeting the needs of the world markets that they had no compunction in neglecting the one market that Government had no right to allow them to neglect - the home market. In order to distribute abroad goods at the cheapest prices compatible with their own profits they regarded cheap labour at home as a necessity. This led to an impoverished home demand. Further, in order to make labour still cheaper, they arranged for cheap foreign food to swamp the home market at the expense of our own agriculture. This led to a further restriction of home demand, the driving of successive generations of British farmers to the wall, and the general decay of the countryside upon whose competence our ancestors had hitherto always been able to sustain life in these islands.

All these things were considered admirable. If the toiling poor complained that they were deplorably treated, they were told in effect that they should be grateful to the lords of industry, who created for them the privilege of being sweated, that they were "the lower orders" and had to learn their station. On the other hand, the moneyed master were told by the well fed philosophers that they were marvellous men - the final objective of the creative force. Herbert Spencer saw in their prosperity confirmation of Darwin's law of the survival of the fittest. They were convinced that when they died they would only have to present personal letters of credit at the Celestial Bank to be admitted into Heaven's most exalted hierarchy. The humanitarian humbug of those times - and not those times alone - served as camouflage to cloak the reality that economic liberalism is a doctrine of stark economic immorality and of disguised slavery that buys men in the cheapest market and sells their output in the dearest.

The system of economic liberalism still prevails in Britain: in a sense more disastrously than ever. But at the same time it is rapidly breaking down. It is breaking down for several reasons, the most immediate being the simple fact - once considered impossible - that Great Britain is no longer the workshop of the world. Other nations long ago decided to manufacture their own goods and to pocket the proceeds. The war accentuated the process. British capital was placed at their disposal for the purpose. In particular, the financiers discovered the productive potentialities of those regions of the world where men are as numerous as weeds, and consequently willing to sell their labour at prices against which not even the British workman can compete. The age is one of mass-production. A Japanese or Chinese or Indian coolie can press a button or pull a lever as efficiently as a man in Lancashire or South Wales. Consequently, goods produced throughout the world by labour still more cheap than our own are succeeding in driving British goods, not only out of our former foreign markets, not only out of our own Imperial markets, but even out of our own home markets. Japanese textiles are being sold in Lancashire, the home of the British textile industry. Czechoslovakian boots and shoes are being sold in Northampton, the home of Britain's footwear industry. Polish coal is being sold in South Wales. And so it is in every other industry. Britain has become the dumping ground of the world, and nearly three million British workers are out of a job in consequence.

The diagnosis of the economic doctors of the old system is "over-production," and in so far as actual production tends to exceed actual purchasing power, their diagnosis is correct. Their treatment, however, is not to bring purchasing power into line with the power to produce, but further to restrict it by driving down British standards even lower in an attempt to regain foreign trade. Apart altogether from its lamentable effect upon home demand, never yet satisfied, this policy postulates a decline instead of an acceleration of world industrialisation and is therefore absurd, even should the British worker be willing to live on a coolie's dish of rice, which he is not. Yet, although British export declines, and must decline (notwithstanding temporary fluctuations), whatever economic system operates, the great banking and financial houses, in concert with every other interest vested in foreign trade, cry aloud for its recapture. That is their own solution to a very perilous problem. The politicians - those who have sufficient brains to see that a problem exists - profess the lunatic belief that Britain can be saved by international agreement. The nations are to meet in conference - as they did under Mr. MacDonald's auspices in the Geological Museum - and voluntarily submit to de-industrialisation in order to please Great Britain. That seems to represent the furthest objectives of political thought, even though international management of economic life would require a world parliament to control prices, regulate raw materials, and equalise wage levels all over the globe. The Labour Party, attached as it is to the system of economic liberalism, seems to pin its faith to some such Parliament; but, then, it always was a staunch believer in pandemonium. When political and economic absurdities of this kind dominate the national life of Britain it is no wonder that crisis should succeed crisis in rapid succession, threatening extinction. After reading the Fascist alternative, which I now set down, the reader is asked to declare whether there is any extravagance in the claim that between Britain and ruin there stands one man and one alone.

Mosley stigmatises as callous, suicidal, and altogether insane the suggestion that there can be real over-production when millions of the people go short of the essential commodities of life. He stresses the fact that there is today no fundamental problem of production, because that problem has been solved by science. The problem is one of distribution. At the same time he derides the notion that distribution can be secured, in the present state of social evolution, by international planning. He describes this as meaning that the British worker must wait for the adequate satisfaction of his needs "until the last Hottentot has joined the

I.L.P." The solution must be a national, or at any rate an imperial solution. This is how, in effect, he approaches the problem:-

Suppose that the rest of the world, apart from the British Empire, were suddenly submerged in the sea, would the people of the Empire be able to sustain life at existing levels? The answer, based on scrupulous research and never once denied by any economist, is that the Empire can produce a sufficiency of raw materials of every kind (apart from a few minor chemicals) not only to maintain present standards, but immeasurably to raise them - enough raw materials, indeed, to abolish poverty forever. The Empire, then, can yield a sufficiency of primary products to give everybody a reasonable share of the raw materials of wealth. What of the finished articles? Is there sufficient manpower available to work on those raw materials and turn them into manufactured goods? In Britain alone there are three million unwillingly idle people eating their hearts out for the opportunity. Possessing the raw materials and the men to work on them, what more is required? A demand for the goods which could be produced. Does the demand exist? Unless the reader be a millionaire he will answer, "Yes" from his own position alone. However moderately well-to-do he may be, there are certain to be many purchases he would like to make, thereby creating employment, if only he had the money, and if that be true of the £250 a year man, or the £500 a year man, or the £2,000 a year man, how much more is it true of the millions of families in this country living near the starvation line? If only a fraction of the present potential demand for goods were added to the present actual demand the whole of the unemployed would be reabsorbed into the economic life of the country. Why, then, are the people not given the extra purchasing power? Why have they not enough money (which is not wealth, but only a token of wealth) to buy the goods they need and which they are able to produce in abundance from an abundant supply of raw materials?

There are two main reasons. First, money has become a bankers' monopoly, to be used primarily for the profit of financial interests and not for the welfare of the community. Money is made cheap or dear at the caprice of the banks, and huge amounts which should be in circulation are either idle in the vaults or sent abroad as loans to finance our competitors against us in the fierce struggle for economic survival. The people have no control whatever over the national credit which their own labour creates.

The second reason is - export trade. Labour at home must be paid the lowest possible wage in order that British goods may compete for foreign markets. In return cheap foreign goods pour into the home market to undercut the British workman. The economic snake thus eats its own confounded tail, because if there is an unfavourable balance of trade the surplus purchasing power is distributed abroad.

Mosley cuts through these chaotic absurdities by declaring that under Fascism British labour will work on British raw materials to produce all the goods that the British people can consume. Foreign products must, therefore, be excluded from these shores. Advantage will then be taken of this exclusion, which will insulate British labour from foreign competition, to reorganise British industry to serve, not the export trade, but an expanded home market. The home market will be expanded by a scientific wage system which equates purchasing power with power to produce. In other words, whatever goods are produced - and production will be maximal in relation to maximal demand - will be sold, because high wages will arm the people of Britain with the money wherewith they will be bought.

The economics of poverty, for the first time in history, will be replaced by the economics of plenty, and no economist will be suffered to talk about "over-production" so long as there is a single demand left unsatisfied.

As protection against external competition is essential for the success of Mosley's policy - a high wage system without it would be a dream - so does Mosley insist upon the abolition of all internal competition which is not strictly qualitative. A firm will be permitted to compete by rendering better services to the customer, but it will not be permitted to secure advantages by price-cutting, which indirectly depresses the wage-level by depressing prices, or by depressing the wage-level through direct means familiar to many generations of workers. So long as either form of competition is allowed, there can never be built up an adequate home market (because an adequate home market demands high wages), and poverty, insecurity, and want will continue to exist. On the other hand, prices will be controlled sufficiently to ensure that they do not leap-frog wages in the usual *laissez-faire* fashion.

This system is known as autarchy, or economic nationalism. It suppresses the economic brigandage of the present system. It allows maximal production to take place, because it facilitates maximal consumption, and refuses to allow the effective power of the nation to consume to be jeopardised by the present dictatorship of vested interests. It ensures a reasonable share of wealth for every individual who works, and in Fascist Britain there will be no room for the work-shy.

Let us see how Mosley proposes to operate his system. He starts with the banks and other financial houses, laying down the first essential - that British credit must be used for British needs and under the direction of the British people, through a mechanism which will be described in the next chapter. Then he comes to the British countryside, so long and grievously neglected by successive Governments. Mosley is confident that the soil of Britain can be made to double its yield in five years. Land banks will be established to assist its intensive cultivation, and for the first time in a hundred years the British farmer will enjoy the British market, whereas today all that he enjoys is the British Marketing Board. The purchasing power now sent abroad in return for foodstuffs will thus be available for our own agricultural community, to the direct benefit of our industries in general. Countryside supplying to the towns will buy from the towns in return. There will follow an immediate industrial revival. Agricultural production will be planned to prevent waste. As the productivity of the land is increased from year to year by reorganisation, so will foreign foodstuffs be commensurately barred admittance.

This does not mean that Britain will become self-supporting. That is an impossibility. But we shall look for the balance, not to foreigners, but to the nations of the Empire. The British farmer will be given the first preference; the second preference will go to the Dominions and Crown Colonies. Because of the exclusion of the foreigner, and because of the high purchasing power of the people - an integral part of Mosley's system - the Empire will enjoy a larger market than it does today; a market sufficiently large to compel Dominion acquiescence and co-operation in economic planning for mutual benefit. The distribution of the wealth of the British Empire will make possible an extremely high standard of living.

While thus planning agricultural production Mosley intends to apply the same principle to manufactured goods. No article which British workmen can produce will be permitted import. Industry will be compensated for whatever losses are incurred in any accelerated decline of the export trade by the rapid expansion of Home and Imperial demands.

Certain industries in Mosley's view require specific provisions. Indian production of raw materials, for instance, will receive every assistance and will enjoy a great Imperial market; but not Indian manufacture. The cotton market will be reserved for Lancashire, as the Crown Colony markets in general will be reserved for British manufactured goods instead of being swamped by those from Japan and other low-wage countries. On the same principle, the home demand for coal will be raised out of all reckoning by compulsory production of oil from coal, to the exclusion of imported petrol. So far as is nationally and Imperially expedient British sources alone will be used for British needs. Mosley is determined that labour shall receive the same treatment. As British goods will be carried only in British ships, so will British ships be allowed to carry only British crews. No foreigner, moreover, will be allowed to enter Britain to perform work which could be performed equally well by a British subject.

What objections are raised to this policy of economic insulation? None that are valid. The most familiar is that it will lead to war. People who for years have purported to find the cause of war in the scramble for international markets now turn round and declare that war will come as a result of withdrawal from the scramble. The argument is absurd. By refusing needless world competition, Fascist economics are a guarantee of peace rather than a cause of war, and, as such, they are now countenanced by great experts like Keynes.

17 - The Corporate Structure

The consistency with which Mosley has sought the fulfilment of the same principles through various media gives authority to his conviction that a new political system is essential to carry through a planned national economy. Parliament in its present form is grotesquely inadequate for the task. Not only is its machinery slow and cumbrous - Mosley often points out that two major measures a year tax its capacity to the uttermost - but the entire system of which it forms a part is designed to leave real power in the hands of minority interests operating from without, thus ensuring the subordination of political control to factions able to exert the strongest economic leverage. Governments come and go but the centres of financial power remain constant, make their peace or pay the penalty. That the great financial houses are able to inflict this penalty nobody who understands existing conditions will deny. The facility with which exchanges may be rigged and money scares created has become notorious - which explains why Government is reluctant to prevent national resources being used largely for the benefit of international money juggling cliques. The public, moreover, has tried every opportunity since the War to observe how Parliamentary democracy enables tight-fisted Lancashire magnates to evade promises to rationalise the cotton industry, or obdurate mine-owners to sabotage each piece of legislative machinery for securing order in the coal industry. Any threat to one complex of interests is interpreted as a threat to the entire body of vested interests dominating the democratic world, and Parliament is the first line of defence to be manned, first because most members belong to the "class" which has always claimed to exercise the privilege of wealth irrespective of any other consideration, and, secondly, because the other less fortunate members have a very marked respect for the powers of defence and counter-attack possessed by the capitalist system. The best men do not come to the top under a system which demands the agility of a tight-rope walker in its successful employment, and even if they did they could not remain the best men long. Compliance with the capitalist racket is the price every democrat must pay for his success, and compliance here spells corruption in its most subtle and devastating sense.

Mosley, therefore, throws scorn on every suggestion that the politicians are capable of planning the nation's economy. That his scorn is justified becomes apparent after a glance even at the futile attempts of Mr. Elliot to look after agriculture in direct opposition to Mr. Runciman, who is trying to foster foreign trade, and even more to Mr. Chamberlain, who is very efficiently looking after the foreign bondholders of the City of London. Planned economy under parliamentary democracy would be planned poverty, because the State would find itself called in to hold the ring still more meticulously for the big financial and industrial interests in their rampage at the expense of the consumers who form the bulk of the nation.

The Fascist leader insists, as a first essential, upon the need for an entirely new political concept to implement the new economic concepts outlined in the previous chapter. He demands recognition of the fact that national planning is an infinitely complex business - much more complex than a surgical operation, which requires and is accorded the co-operation of everybody concerned. Party politicians and big-scale capitalists, on becoming surgical cases, would be outraged if at the moment of their operation the anaesthetist demanded a larger commission, or if the medical students grappled with the surgeon for the possession of his knife, or if the surgeon held the patient up to ransom for a higher fee, or if interminable committee meetings were held to debate where the incision should be made, or if the nurses refused to move before ventilating a grievance, or if the matron decided to throw a fit of hysterics in the best *News Chronicle* manner. In so far as the patients were politicians and financiers so lawless a system might justify itself, although they would be the last to see it in that light. Yet these would be much the same chaotic and lunatic methods as those they employ in their treatment of the nation they are supposed to serve. That is why Great Britain has entered into a decline which, unchecked, must lead to the death of all her greatness.

Mosley sees clearly that the task of securing economic sanity can only be carried out if the Government is given power to act, which means that it must be able to command the absolute co-operation of all sections of the community instead of being subjected to the expedients of obstruction and sabotage which powerful minorities so dextrously use to their own advantage at the present time. He will come to the people of Britain at a General Election, therefore, and place at their disposal the tempered weapon of his Blackshirt movement for carrying out in government the programme which he has presented to them. If the British electorate prefer to carry on with the present game of bluff, in which political promises are made merely to be broken, and in which the great combines continue to exert their stranglehold on the nation, then they will reject the Fascist candidates and financial democracy will enjoy a renewed lease of life. On the other hand, should the British people give their mandate to Mosley and his Blackshirts they will allow no force on earth - no financial conspiracy, no mass attack of capitalism, no Press rampage, no frame-up by a corrupt Trade Unionism - to stand between the people and the fulfilment in action of their will. That is what is meant by Fascist Dictatorship - a Dictatorship of the will of the nation in place of the existing Dictatorship of Vested Interests suborning democracy to their frequently outrageous purposes.

Reactionaries who believe that the people of Britain are so run-to-seed that they can be frightened by words make much use of this word "dictatorship" in their effort to discredit Mosley and his policy, affirming that he seeks to destroy - what is also only a word today - their "liberty." Should Britons, indeed, have become so woolly-minded as to think in terms of words instead of realities they will prove themselves unworthy of Fascism, and there will be nothing to prevent their suffering the "liberty" to go increasingly short of commodities in a time of abundance, to live in ever more extensive slums, and to see a banker's ramp break up forever all that there has been in our islands of majestic purpose and great endeavour. But Mosley has sufficient faith in the British people to know that they will not tolerate the continued betrayal of national interests once they understand the exact nature of the Fascist alternative. The assertion that Mosley wishes to abolish liberty is dishonest and absurd. His desire is to give people liberty - real liberty to enjoy the wealth that science enables them to produce, liberty to live in a decent, self-respecting country where there shall be sun and air and health for all, liberty to go their ways in peace without being followed by grandmotherly legislators, liberty to take part in the corporate life of a resurgent and vital Empire. The only liberty he denies is the liberty of anti-social factions to exploit the community for their own purposes.

Once returned to power Mosley will ask Parliament to pass a General Powers Bill, which Fascist Government will use to introduce more essential legislation in six months than could be negotiated through the present system in as many years. Work will be put immediately in hand for building up the vast home market which forms the cornerstone of his economic policy. During the transitionary period vast relief schemes will be started to prepare the way for full Fascist economic planning. The might of the nation will be mobilised to obliterate the disgrace of the slums, to place electric power at the disposal of all, to build vast roads, to reclaim land from the sea, to do the hundreds of jobs that cry aloud to be done. Vested interests which stand athwart the nation's path will be smashed.

While these projects are being advanced the long-term policy of industrial and agricultural reorganisation will be introduced as rapidly as possible. The finest brains in the country will be employed for the purpose. The new education will come into being and with it a new spirit of devotion to the constructive tasks of peace. Measures protecting the people against anti-social ramps, corrupt practices, and economic non-co-operation will speedily pass into law. Offenders will be treated by the Courts as ordinary felons. The long reign of economic plunder and political humbug will be brought abruptly to an end.

No liberty will be held forfeit which advances the cause of national well-being and happiness. Liberty that fails to come within this scope will be regarded as license and destroyed. The Press will have every freedom except the license to mislead the public or to create a panic or to offend against national self-respect. Newspaper directors and editors may do as they please, but there will be imposed upon them by law a sense of responsibility, because every lie, every distortion, every piece of unwarranted sensationalism that they publish may well see them securely lodged in jail. So with the "intellectuals." They will enjoy every opportunity of offering constructive criticism, but not the opportunity to obstruct. The time is past when a great nation can afford to be stampeded in any anti-social direction that happens to suit selfish interests. The new era of economic and political sanity demands the discipline of unity and reason.

Mosley insists upon this power to act, but he does not propose that it should be independent of subsequent public control. His system can succeed only if the overwhelming majority of his countrymen give it their enthusiastic help, and accordingly it is his intention to make provision for consulting the people by means of direct plebiscite on every issue of paramount importance for their welfare outside the general mandate accorded him at the elections. Moreover, it shall always be possible for Parliament to dismiss Government by a vote of censure. After the first parliamentary period, however, party politics as such will cease to exist. The problems of the age, Mosley stresses, are technical problems to be solved by technicians. By regarding them as political problems the door is left open for vested interests again to assert their domination behind the familiar facade of facile electoral promises. On that account democratic representation must be transferred from an amateur to a specialist basis.

Here Mosley challenges the whole theory implicit in the present system of parliamentary democracy. That theory assumes - or pretends to assume - the equal ability of all citizens to base their votes upon informed opinions. The assumption is dangerous and false. The average individual has the haziest views on most of the highly complicated matters which engage the attention of modern government. His education provides him with little relevant data. Even if he possessed that data, the concealment of the real issues even from Parliament, and the further distortions of the Press, leave him in complete ignorance of what is actually happening behind the scenes. As it is, democracy boils down to a system whereby millions of people are stampeded in this or that direction over issues which they do not understand, and which, in any event, are not the real issues. In order to understand Mosley's approach to this important problem it is necessary for some test questions to be asked. How many farm labourers can truthfully declare that they know sufficient economics to pass a sound judgement on the workings of the Gold Standard? How many doctors can place a finger on the fundamental fallacies of Douglas Social Credit? How many carpenters are able to discuss the Eisler currency proposals, or to advance a claim that they have even heard of them? How many clerks, or architects, or shopkeepers can speak with authority on invisible imports, or give an enlightened opinion on the effect of the Bank of England monopoly? Yet democracy postulates the existence of this knowledge and with it the individual's control over the whole field of community life - a postulate which ensures that he shall possess no control whatever, since in every department of knowledge there are men who understand precisely what is involved and do not hesitate to exploit the general ignorance of the electorate. Democracy, in other words, is an instrument for fooling all the people all the time.

This is not to say that the electorate is incompetent to take its part in the national councils. Survival demands that it be given the earliest possible opportunity to do so. But its contribution must be rescued from the unreality of the present democratic system and guided along specialist channels to the services of the community. There is always one sphere in which every man is to greater or lesser extent a specialist, and that is the sphere of his own trade or profession. The farm labourer may not understand the Gold Standard, but he does understand farming to the full extent of his intelligence and experience. So with the doctor, the carpenter, the architect, and the rest. They all know a good deal about their own jobs. These considerations have led Mosley to propose the replacement of the geographical by the occupational franchise. The citizens of any given town will cease to vote, let us say, for a retired colonel or soap manufacturer to represent their geographical interests - which as a rule do not exist - upon issues only partially revealed to them, and which their representatives cannot handle in their interests without incurring the displeasure of the Party machine - a risk they prove themselves singularly unwilling to accept. Instead, farm labourers will be represented by a farm labourer; doctors by a doctor; and so on throughout the whole occupational field. Thus, the members of every trade and profession will be vitally represented by practical men and women who understand their needs and the needs of their calling, and Parliament will become a workshop in which every phase of national activity is accorded an effective voice, instead of being composed of hordes of lawyers and party hacks who understand very little about anything except duty to their own careers.

During the first five years, while the processes of transformation are being prepared, Members of Parliament will be obliged to relinquish their role as chatterers and obstructionists; they will be sent back to their constituencies to help forward the policies for which the people as a whole have voted.

Even when Parliament is reformed, however, it will not be considered the most suitable assembly to undertake the exacting labours of national economic planning. The task is too vast and complex to be discharged either from Westminster or from

Whitehall, and here we come to a consideration of the basic structure of the Fascist state as an alternative both to *laissez-faire* Democracy and to Communism. While Socialists of the various international schools are hopelessly disunited as to method, those who have any kind of definite objective advocate the ultimate merging of private into public enterprise. They adhere to the principle of national ownership. The creed of National Socialism - that is, the Fascist creed - denies the desirability of so extreme a measure, and affirming that socialisation is impotent to make unprofitable enterprises profitable, and arguing that instead of increasing efficiency its effect is inevitably the opposite, since the entire emphasis in a Socialist State must be placed continuously upon production - as we have seen in Russia - whereas under private enterprise no such stress is required. Private enterprise has already solved the problem of production. The problem which it has disastrously failed to solve is that of distribution, but to suppose that it must be abolished on that account is very much like insisting that because motor cars lead to accidents they must be driven off the roads in order that everybody may be crammed into one huge State omnibus. This analogy serves well to illustrate the Socialist position. Moreover, in so far as the Socialists declare themselves convinced democrats, it will be seen that they make provision for the omnibus passengers to fight as much as they please among themselves and to wrestle continuously with the driver for possession of the steering wheel. Parliamentary democracy makes a lamentable show even in dealing within its present scope: imagination boggles at the thought of the disaster it would contrive if it were to be given possession of the nation's entire design for living.

It is not surprising, therefore, to find Mosley setting his face against the abolition of private enterprise. What he advocates is not social ownership, but social control. Men will be allowed to enrich themselves - but only as a reward for services to the community. They must at every turn subordinate their interests to the national interest, and should they fail to do so, violating the special laws introduced by Fascism, society will not hesitate to express its displeasure through His Majesty's judges. Economic plunderers will no longer escape the consequences of actions incalculably more anti-social than those of thieves who steal a few pounds and go to gaol. It is through the relentless control of private enterprise and the widest possible distribution of private property that National Socialism will achieve its end and solve the problem of the maldistribution of goods which perpetuates poverty in the wealthiest Empire in the history of the world.

In building up the structure to take over this power of control Mosley is able to give practical shape to his old dream - expressed, as we saw, at Harrow - of incorporating the great legitimate interests of labour as partners in the nation's organic life. The Fascist Corporate State makes fundamental provision for this partnership. As political control will rest upon an occupational basis in Parliament, so will economic control rest upon an occupational basis in the actual industries. That is, instead of being centralised in London, economic planning will become the function of industrial self-government. In each industry the employers will be organised in their own special trade unions. Each trade union will link up with its opposite number among the employers' associations to form a corporation on which the consumers' interests will be represented by Government nominees. It will be the job of these corporations to regulate the entire activities of the industries with which they are concerned - to plan production and distribution, to prevent anti-social competition, to lower prices as circumstances permit, to raise wages by express policy, and to set the general tone of their own industrial life. The measures passed by them will have the force of law - subject to approval by the National Council of Corporations. This body, consisting of representatives of all the corporations, will review such legislation in its relation to the national interest and will be charged with the task of securing the balanced economy that Fascism requires. Herein will be found exposure of another piece of democratic misrepresentation - the lie that Mosley intends to destroy the trade unions. His intention is precisely the reverse. He proposes to eliminate their corrupt leadership, it is true, but the unions themselves will be elevated to a position of equal partnership with employers in industry, with an equal voice in laying down its broad principle of conduct.

The nation's finances will be organised as an integral part of the corporate system. Mosley proposes a Finance Corporation to regulate general banking and insurance activities; with a National Investment Board, working in conjunction with the National Corporation of Industry, to relate the operations of British finance to the needs of British industry. He lays down the Fascist principle on this subject at some length in "The Greater Britain," in the course of which he writes: "It must be a fundamental axiom of Fascism that high finance, like every other interest within the State, must be subordinated to the policy of the State, and must serve the welfare of the nation as a whole. In adopting this position, for the first time in British politics, after the weak surrender of all parties to the power of finance, the British Government would have the overwhelming support of the mass of the people, both worker and employer, whose productive efforts have been frustrated by the policy of high finance. The attitude of the City itself will determine the need, or otherwise, for intervention. Indeed, within the City itself considerable support could be found for this position from genuine British and patriotic elements, who are not enmeshed in the trammels of foreign finance. Let us hope that it may prove possible, by co-operation with such elements in the City, to secure the co-operation of British finance in a planned economy of national reconstruction. Otherwise the Gordian knot must be cut.

Many of our recent troubles have arisen from the fact that our financial system has grown up in a tradition of international rather than British finance. The business of the great finance houses has been largely foreign business, rather than the supply of finance to British industry. This tradition has a natural origin in the fact that British industry originally itself financed new developments chiefly from its own resources and reserves, and without much recourse to the City.

17 - The Corporate Structure

However, that epoch has long passed away, and urgent measures of big-scale rationalisation seek financial aid, only to find the whole practice, tradition and interest of the City engaged in international finance. The big banks have developed also a tradition of rigorously refraining from industrial enterprise, and content themselves with advances upon collateral security, irrespective of the purpose to which the borrower will devote the credit...... It is vitally necessary to provide a banking machinery for the re-equipment of British industry. Hitherto, Government has washed its hands of one of the major problems of the age, and has abdicated in favour of the Bank of England, which in equipment, training and tradition was manifestly unsuited to the task, while on general grounds of administrative principle the Central Bank does not seem to be the appropriate instrument for the details of industrial reconstruction. "The result, after three years' experience, has so far produced no noticeable improvement in the conditions of British industry. Hitherto the power of finance in industry has been used, not so much to produce efficiency and to promote new enterprises, as to maintain concerns which were demonstrably rotten, long after their economic basis had gone, in the hope of ultimately liquidating ill judged credits which were frozen."

This, then, is a brief outline of the Fascist system - retention in political control of electoral representation, transferred from a regional to a vocational basis, and the introduction of representation into the sphere of economic control. But it will be a new kind of democratic representation, engaged with technical realities, and not with the corrupt sham-fights of the Party game. Over and above all other bodies, and subject only to His Majesty the King, will be the dynamic force of the Fascist Government, Court of Appeal against injustice, inspirator of the corporate life of the people, custodian of national values, watchdog of the new civilisation. Fascist Government, elected by the people through direct plebiscite, will be answerable only to King and people, whereas democratic Governments answer only to those sectional interest who pay the piper and call the tune. Electoral representation, in its new specialist orientation, will play a great part in the national assemblies; but one anticipates that the British nation will soon discover that the finest and truest representation is to chose a great leader of intelligence, courage and integrity and give him the power to act in accordance with an approved programme, but with an absolute discretion as to the ways and means. Fascism stands or falls by the leadership principle, which is inherent throughout nature. Committees and assemblies and parliaments may be so constituted that they do not betray community interests; but the best government, the only really responsible government, is that of a great man who is devoted to his country and his cause, and who is able to call upon the best brains in the land for co-operation and advice. Therefore, under Fascism, there will always be found a responsible national leader subject to the King. His Government will withdraw progressively from active intervention as the corporate system begins to function, but his presence will always be felt as an inspiring force that will not fail to act when the occasion requires and take full responsibility for his actions. Precisely the same principle will be applied to Local Government, the super structure of which is frequently almost eaten away by graft. Every town will be run by a leader, assisted by elected councillors, but individually responsible to the Government for its sound management.

Such in general are Mosley's proposals for the introduction of Fascist method into Britain. They constitute the sole terms on which he would consent to take over the reins of power. The representational safeguard is absolute. At the same time, once Fascism assumes control it will brook no interference while it gets on with the job, since only at the end of the usual parliamentary periods will the electors be free to get rid of it. During the intervals the economic and political dog fights will be brought to an end and every citizen required to lend his full weight to the building of a greater Britain. A moment's thought should convince the reader that on no other terms could an honest leader undertake the responsibility of attempting to rescue the country from its present plight.

18 - The Philosophy Of Fascism

Because of the insistence placed by Mosley on the subordination of sectional interests to the national interest, he is accused, in line with other Fascist leaders, of exalting the State above the individual. It is an absurd criticism, because, rightly considered, the State is no other than the whole body of individuals subject to one government, so that every emphasis put upon the welfare of the State is an emphasis placed upon the welfare of the people composing the State. Indeed; it is the negation of this principle implicit in the concept of the State as standing apart from, and even hostile to, the welfare of the individual which has led to the neglect of almost every community interest during the rise of European Liberalism, which still holds Britain in its clutch. A philosophy which reads into the commercial rampage and industrial tyranny of the last century and of today the law of the survival of the fittest can scarcely be expected to encourage the idea of State responsibility for the mass of the people. The old individualist view of the State as the chief agent of tyranny has become insupportable; today an alert and scientific State is seen by increasing numbers of individuals to be their chief bulwark, since in the absence of State regulation they are completely at the mercy of the combines and trusts and newspapers. Even capitalism begins to discern in its agency a power able to yield more positive service than merely to keep the ring for *laissez-faire* capitalist activities, with the result that there is some kind of State-planning for production or not infrequently to discourage production. When the people of Britain discover the uses of the State in the same way there will be Fascist planning for distribution. In fact, from whatever angle it is approached, the State can no longer be regarded as a purely passive factor in the economic struggle.

Fascism, it is true, does not stop at building a corporate structure whereby the nation's economic life may be regulated, because it is not merely in the economic sphere that the individuals composing the State are oppressed and cheated out of the fullness of life. There is, in the Fascist view, an obligation to look after the spirit no less than the body of the nation. Not only does it insist, for example, that individualism should be guided along socially advantageous channels, but that the greatest effort should be made to "condition" individuals, so that they no longer desire to pursue anti-social activities. This raises a mighty Liberal outcry. "Conditioning" is regarded by them as an unwarrantable interference with the sacredness of human personality. Here, as everywhere else, however, Liberal philosophy is concerned more with its own fictions than with realities.

Human beings are "conditioned" in any case, whether they are aware of it or not, and whether they like it or not. At the present time they arrive at manhood firmly convinced that what the world requires of them is success, and that success is to be measured by money. The heroes of the democratic world are not its prophets, its poets, its unselfish leaders (if they exist under democracy), its strugglers, its splendid failures, but its flamboyantly successful individuals, its millionaires. Young people whose lives are lived instinctively absorb from their environment this stark materialism of the age, and all their own values in course of time become money values. The youth becomes aware that by his own success or failure as a money-getter will the bourgeois world judge him. His eligibility as a suitor will consist, at any rate, in some part, of his worth in money. His happiness in marriage will possibly hinge upon much the same factor, because if his wife upholds bourgeois standards she will wish to appear at least as affluent as her next-door neighbour. Should he have social ambition he finds that his social value is almost always his cash value. What the instinctive individual does more or less unconsciously the more thoughtful individual does with set purpose. Arriving at the threshold of life with his eyes open the thoughtful young man sees clearly what is expected of him and studies the careers of his exemplars, learning how egotism, ruthlessness and sharp practice all take their part in the making of a bourgeois hero. He realises that if he plays his own cards with due care and in conformity with certain rules there is almost no anti-social economic activity which it will not pay him to pursue, and the larger the scale of that activity the less likely is he to find himself in gaol, and the more likely to find himself in time a respected member of the House of Lords. Fascism will reverse these possibilities, but instead of putting successful men in gaol for what will be regarded as crimes against the nation's economic life, how much greater a thing will it be to lead the mind and spirit of man into a new orientation, with service instead of money as the new value?

That is the main revolution which Fascism seeks to achieve - a revolution destroying the bourgeois concepts of monetary success and other meretricious values in order to harness the devotion of the people to the building up of a society without class barriers, in which every individual instinctively harmonises his own interests within the confines of the general community interest. To establish a great revolution of this kind - the only kind of revolution which can give dignity, poise, and an assured survival-basis to the nation - it will be necessary to employ every resource of the human brain that can help to create an atmosphere in which the "conditioning" may take effect. They say, the enemies of Fascism, that its aim is a standardised race of people, with a standardised slave mentality. No suggestion could be more fatuous. The Fascist desires the fullest development of the industrial personality; the greatest flowering of human genius; the highest employment of every talent; all the splendour of man's diversified skill. These things today are crushed beneath the incubus of bourgeois rapacity and humbug. The bourgeois mind, therefore must be educated out of existence, and every interim manifestation of its more criminal tendencies ruthlessly suppressed in order that the spirit of Britain may be freed from its preoccupation with a needless insecurity and wretchedness, and released for the greater adventures of high corporate endeavour. To this end education will be used with unremitting vigour to create a spirit in which high purposes will no longer be considered a subject for scorn, but the only road to advancement and prestige in the Fascist State. "Opportunity will be open to all; privilege to none," declares Mosley. A man's measure will be the measure of his service, not the measure of his bank account. If classes must always to some extent exist, Fascism is determined that there shall be no arbitrary class barriers, and that the greatest positions in the State shall be granted to the men and women of the most solid worth and ability, whatever their origins, and not to the merely "high born," the slick and the plausible.

Anti-Fascists declare that these things are contrary to human nature; they affirm that man will do nothing unless there be personal gain or kudos attached to it. This is true only of the slaves of bourgeois-democratic "morality." In general it is a damnable lie and slander. Men did not expose themselves to the agonies of stomach wounds to impress their next-door neighbours. Mosley and the other leaders of the modern movement have seen something of the real sublimity of mankind, and it is the knowledge that this capacity for superb and selfless achievement is available for the constructive tasks of peace which is at once the spiritual basis and the inspiration of Fascism.

Nevertheless, Mosley turns no blind eye to other human impulses and motives. It is only from those dedicated to the Fascist struggle and the Fascist life, his own followers, that he demands the uttermost devotion to the cause and expects that final surrender to its need in which self is absorbed in service. He recognises that it is natural in man to desire to fend for himself and for his family, and regards this as an entirely healthy instinct so long as it is not perverted by the corrupt atmosphere of materialism into anti-social channels. Laws will be laid down for the absolute protection of the communal interest, but so long as he obeys those laws the individual may enrich himself as much as he pleases, because in doing so he will enrich the whole nation by his initiative and toil. He will hold his wealth, however, on trust for national uses. As he will not be allowed to make money by actions harmful to the public, so will he be forbidden to spend or otherwise employ money to the public detriment. Capital, like land, like factories, like all other possessions, may be privately owned but there will be no absolute right in such ownership except through conformity with national needs and observance of corporative laws.

In the same way Mosley recognises that it is natural for man to work that his children may benefit by his exertions, and on that account it will be permissible for possessions to be handed down to the next generation, which will be similarly required to make beneficial use of them for the community. But to the next generation only. The sons will hand down to their sons only the results of their own labour; death duties will claim the rest for the nation. Neither will the inheritance of wealth continue to create an exclusive, privileged class, because for the able child there will be free educational facilities through every stage of school, college, university, and even beyond, in order that the nation may be served by the best brains and the best technicians it can produce. Moreover, there will be no wealth without service, and therefore no idle rich.

In order to achieve a collective life inspired by these ideals there will be required an entirely new educational approach and an intensive training of the young in the new concepts of civic duty and of nationhood, It would be unreasonable to suppose that having created the new education Fascism would be content to see these finer values systematically destroyed by sub-men battering on our cultural life and debasing it for their own profit. While every phase of Britain's industrial and commercial life will require regulation in order to distribute the national wealth, no less attention will be paid to the nation's spiritual wealth, which at present is dissipated in the service of purely parasitical interests. Thus Mosley is determined that the Press under Fascism shall be an inspiration to the nation and not a source of corruption as it is today. In the first place men whose job it is to sell news to the public will find themselves in a Court of Law, facing a charge of false pretences, should they sell lies. Every Press Lord and every editor will be held personally and jointly responsible for the truth or falsity of the news published.

Secondly, the power of the Press to stampede public opinion in the interests of sectional interests seeking to regain their old dominion will be ruthlessly suppressed. Thirdly, it will be a criminal offence for newspapers to blackguard foreign rulers and foreign nations, thereby safeguarding the world against irresponsible wars brought on by the screeches of hysterical jackasses of the *News Chronicle* and *Daily Herald* type. Finally, the pouring into the public mind, day after day, and year after year, of all the sickly "sensation" and other maladies of a spiritually disordered underworld will be given the closest scrutiny with a view to eliminating as far as possible every degrading feature of the Press which now impoverishes the national life. Initiative will be taken by Fascist Government wherever intervention is required, but most of it will come from within the profession. Journalists for years have been clamouring for the reform and better ordering of the Press, but under the present system lack the means to do more than pass futile resolutions at their annual conferences. Under Fascism they will be given what Mosley calls "power-action" to put their house in order and give Britain newspapers of which it may be proud.

So, too, will it be in the theatre and cinema worlds. One of the first duties of Fascism will be to recapture the British cinema and the British theatre for the British nation. The alien stranglehold will be broken and the cosmopolitan mass-production of shoddy, demoralising and narcotic plays and films brought to an end, in order that the finest creative genius and artistic talent of Britain may find its true expression independently of present day box-office assessments and in service to the ideal of enriching the life of a great people.

In the same way, building a nobler Britain will not permit the preaching of any creed which obstructs that work or encourages young manhood to look upon its defence as a matter beneath their notice and contempt. Pacifism - the gospel of decadence - will be wiped out of existence. In the event of this country or the Empire being attacked, every man will be compelled to play a part in repelling the invader. Men who lack the manhood to take up arms in the hour of danger lack the manhood to make any contribution of value when the danger hour is passed and peace restored. Their influence must therefore be destroyed. That extremely brilliant Fascist writer, William Joyce, has summed up the Fascist attitude towards the conscientious objector in his definition: "A pacifist, being unwilling to risk danger in defence of his land, is lower than the lowest kind of protoplasmic life known to science." But that is the only call to arms Fascism would ever make. Mosley has given his solemn pledge that never again will British blood be shed in a foreign quarrel or for any purpose except the defence of British soil.

In general, therefore, it will be seen that there are certain "liberties" which Fascism curtails, but that these "liberties" are inherently disintegrating and inimical to real freedom - the freedom to live and work and enjoy and serve. Mosley lays it down that in private life the people under Fascism will have every reasonable liberty and will be released from the innumerable petty restrictions and tyrannies of the present day, but that in public life their every action must be framed in accordance with a sense of responsibility to the nation.

It will be noticed, too, that the Fascist stress is placed quite unashamedly on the national welfare in an epoch which professes concern only for international welfare. That is because Fascism is a realist creed. Time and again during his career Mosley has pointed out the absurdity of international economic planning so long as each nation is in a different stage of economic development and to a greater or less degree subject to the caprice of its own dominant vested interests. Not until every nation has replaced economic ruthlessness by economic law within its own frontiers will international economic law and order be anything more than a dream, and every attempt to secure it an ugly dream. Finance having broken through national frontiers to obtain a wider field for its rampage, its idealistic dupes follow behind unwittingly trailing a smokescreen to hide its activities, and shouting their parrot cries in praise of Geneva and Collective Security in pathetic ignorance that they are helping to fashion an instrument whereby financial democracy hopes to destroy its opponent, the modern movement, in a world war.

It is not alone for economic reasons that Fascism is strongly nationalist. It recognises that nations exist no matter to what extent their existence may displease H.G. Wells and his friends. The most truly universal culture is also the most national culture, because it is to the nation that it owes its landscape and its soil, whereas cosmopolitan cultures are a synthetic, ugly thing without roots - more bastardisations that reduce all things to their own lowest common denominator. The Fascist serves mankind through service to his own nation, whereas the internationalist serves nobody because there is no soil for his growth and no sense of his own national tradition. The latter is content to surrender himself to the unrealities of his own creation; the former builds upon the foundations which exist. Only through nationalism, indeed, can universalism come into being. Mosley expressed this truth superbly in a recent article, in which he wrote: "In the final synthesis while civilisation can discover a comprehensive policy which rests on the reality of mutual interests, and in Europe at least will be infused by the spiritual communion of the world creed of the twentieth century. The system of Financial Democracy crumbles in decay to collapse throughout the world, and the stricken and bewildered peoples search for an alternative which presents hope of peace and security. The alternative of the modern movement rises with the stark realism of granite above the confusion of present politics, not only as a rock on which humanity may build anew, but as a conception illuminated by the highest ideal of national and world citizenship which has yet animated the soul of man. The realism of the new creed builds upon the basic fact of economic settlement and justice for individual nations, without which all else is in vain. It recognises that European leadership must rest with the great Powers, which can guarantee not only the peace of Europe, but the peace of the world once their policies are united in objectives which are susceptible of synthesis. But materialism alone is not enough, and upon the basic fact of an established community of interest the universalism of Fascism and National Socialism erects the majestic edifice of a new world idea which commands the mind and spirit of man with the fiery force of a new religion. The old world and the new world will not mingle: so the peace of mankind attends in all lands the passing of the old world, and Britain, by force of material power and potential of moral leadership becomes the ultimate arena of struggle between the Old and the New within which the destiny of white civilisation will be decided. Great is the responsibility that high fate imposes upon us. We fight not only for the salvation of the land we have; we fight also for the Peace of Mankind."

Mosley perceives in this great modern movement of Fascism a synthesis of what have previously been considered the antithetical creeds of Christianity and Nietzsche. "On the one hand," he has written, "you find in Fascism, taken from Christianity, taken directly from the Christian conception, the immense vision of service, of self-abnegation, of self-sacrifice in the cause of others, in the cause of the world, in the cause of your country; not the elimination of the individual, so much as the fusion of the individual in something far greater than himself; and you have that basic doctrine of Fascism - service, self-surrender - to what the Fascist must conceive to be the greatest cause and the greatest impulse in the world. On the other hand you find taken from Nietzschian thought the virility, the challenge to all existing things which impeded the march of mankind, the absolute abnegation of the doctrine of surrender; the firm ability to grapple with and to overcome all obstructions. You have, in fact, the creation of a doctrine of men of vigour and of self-help, which is the other outstanding characteristic of Fascism."

The animating force which creates and fosters the Fascist way of life has often been called Caesarism. Mosley does not run away from the definition, but insists that it is a collective Caesarism, modern organisation being too vast to rest on any one man alone. "The will and talent of the individual is replaced by the will and ability of the disciplined thousands who comprise a Fascist movement. The organised will of devoted masses, subject to a voluntary discipline, and inspired by the passionate ideal of national survival, replaces the will to power and a higher order of the individual superman." He believes that it may be given to collective Caesarism to establish the fundamentals of collective life for all time, and expresses this thought in a magnificent passage:

"At a moment of great world crisis, a crisis which in the end will inevitably deepen, a movement emerges from a historic background which makes its emergence inevitable, carrying certain traditional attributes derived from a very glorious past, but facing the facts of today armed with the instruments which only this age has ever conferred upon mankind. By this new and wonderful coincidence of instrument and of event the problems of this age can be overcome, and the future can be assured in a progressive stability. Then at long last, 'Caesarism,' the mightiest emanation of the human spirit in high endeavour toward enduring achievement, will have performed its world mission, will have expiated its sacrifice in the struggle of the ages, and will have fulfilled its historic identity. A humanity released from poverty and from many of the horrors and afflictions of disease to the enjoyment of a world reborn through science will still need a Fascist movement transformed to the purpose of a new and nobler order of mankind; but you will need no more the strange and disturbing men who, in the days of struggle and of danger and in nights of darkness and of labour, have forged the instruments of steel by which the world shall pass to higher things."

If the processes of "conditioning" to which reference has been made are ever complete, then Mosley's idea is certainly not too optimistic. More likely is it, in my view, that there will always be need for the "strange and disturbing men," no matter how many problems have been solved, to maintain their posts in the watch-towers of mankind, eternally devoted, eternally vigilant - the sentries who maintain watch and ward over the nation's soul.

19 - Leader Of Men

The reader now possesses in outline an idea of the comprehensive policy for which Mosley battles against the massed might of the old order, wearing every kind of persecution as proudly as a plume. By this time some portrait of him has, perhaps, emerged from these pages - a portrait of his mind with its majestic endowments: his tall athletic frame, with its dynamic force and immense reserves of strength; his unconquerable spirit, with its grandeur of courage and resolve. The portrait, in short, of an outstanding leader of men. It has been shown how loyal he has been to his own principles even when his friends were fewest and his cause at its lowest ebb. We have seen how he has never hesitated to back his own judgement by courses which seemed impossible and absurd to his contemporaries, and to persist along them until hundreds and thousands of men and women have followed him with the absolute conviction that they are the only roads to be pursued if Britain is to live. It has been shown how he has distained the short cuts of the careerist and the crooked ways of the political charlatan: how he has weathered ridicule, violence, and abuse because of the tempered steel of his character, and sacrificed every advantage of wealth and social position in order to take up the hard fight for his native land which for many years has been so cruelly wronged.

Nevertheless, the reader may grant all these things, and yet fall into some of the errors which the newspapers spread as traps to prevent his arriving at a just estimate of this remarkable man. There is, for example, the false picture of him sitting high and inaccessible above the heads of his fellow countrymen, discouraging all relationships with them except to give them orders: proud, dictatorial, harsh, almost misanthropic, concerned only with his own point of view to the exclusion of all others. One has reason to suppose that many people think of Mosley in this way, and here is the most suitable place to put before them what every individual with any knowledge of the man will agree to be a more accurate impression. First of all, let it be explained that Oswald Mosley is a very kind man - far and away the kindest man I know. It is not the vague amiability which so often passes for kindness: there is nothing vague or weak about it. Instead, Mosley's kindness is born of strong, tense, generous emotions of a sense of the innate decency of mankind, of a natural inclination to think well of his fellow men, and of a very profound insight into the mainsprings of human action which enables him to understand when they fail. He is kind even to his enemies. He has lashed Ramsay MacDonald hundreds of times, and that he will continue to do so whenever the need arises one does not doubt, but while he is bitter beyond words about MacDonald the Prime Minister, about MacDonald the man he has nothing very devastating to say. "A nice, woolly old boy," is how I have heard Mosley describe him. Then there is Winston Churchill, with whom he has had so many merciless battles in the House. He does not think of the hard words spoken when his mind dwells upon this very old adversary of his - "Churchill was a very gallant foe," is what he says. Even Thomas is dismissed with a shake of the head, and "I'm afraid I never had any use for Thomas." Mosley has the rare intellectual gift of being able to separate them from their actions, and while he may abominate the latter and go to almost any length to combat them, the former appear very seldom to arouse his hatred. Instead, he goes out of his way to learn the reason why they act as they do.

Since Mosley is thus generous to his opponents, his attitude towards his followers and friends may be predicted. It takes the form of a loyalty stronger and more absolute than the world of democratic politicians would believe possible. Mosley demands loyalty from his associates: otherwise Fascism could not meet the iron-hard necessities of the time. But in return he gives loyalty in the fullest measure. Thus the compact between Leader and followers is of a kind not known among Britons since 1918, and never before known in British politics.

Mosley is also one of the most patient and approachable of men - providing it is not the intention of those who seek interviews to waste time that belongs to Fascism: he has suffered enough from talkers. But nobody who has a view to put forward or a legitimate complaint to make finds it difficult to come face to face with his Leader: it is the privilege of every Fascist in Britain. And every individual who does receive an interview has the satisfaction of knowing that his point has been grasped by the most alert intelligence of modern times. Another absurd supposition is that because Mosley rejects the committee principle he finds his own views self-sufficient. This is entirely untrue. Before coming to decisions it is his invariable practice to consult his senior officers, and they are not only encouraged, but required to say exactly what they have in mind, irrespective of whether or not the views they express coincide with his own. Failure to do so, indeed, is regarded as an offence. Mosley is not irritated when a man disagrees with him, as the old gangs assert. On the contrary, he is eager for helpful criticism. But there is no voting, and the responsibility of the decision is the Leader's alone. That is the greatest improvement on the democratic method not one of those taking part in these conferences would deny, first because Mosley's extraordinary intellectual power often enables him to synthesise what first appear to be conflicting opinions, and second because his own views are almost invariably confirmed by events. Once the decision is given there is no further argument: the ruling does not require to be enforced, because it is instinctively accepted by every officer. That is part of Mosley's real greatness: he has no need to dictate, for the good reason that his spiritual quality precludes the necessity of "laying down the law" to men who share so completely his own outlook and serve him with so large a pride. This is the man of whom the newspapers not long ago were writing that he would never achieve leadership because of his inability to inspire followers. It is true, however, that Mosley does not inspire windbags and opportunists to follow him, which explains another criticism levelled against him - that the men around him for the most part were not previously in the public eye: they were not "well-known." That cannot be gainsaid, because it is a lamentable fact that those who achieve success under democracy stick to it like leeches even though large numbers of them are known privately to despise the system which they operate. In the old world of political expediency it is not to be expected that many will be found willing to jeopardise their careers and sacrifice present rewards to accept the hard and even desperate fight to which Mosley's life has been dedicated. They prefer to wait before "conversion" overtakes them, little guessing that then it will be too late. Mosley is not battling to wrench Britain from the control of the cowardly and incompetent merely for the pleasure of handing it back to them when the battle has been won.

Already the services he has rendered through Fascism in Britain and to the world have been of incalculable value. When the Jews were at the height of their campaign to drag this country into war with Germany, his voice alone was raised to express the desire of the British nation to live at peace with that great people, and in their counter-campaign the Blackshirts entirely restored the balance and defeated the ends of Jewish propaganda. Again, in the splurge of democratic folly which led to the imposition of sanctions against Italy, Mosley used his organisation in a mighty and successful effort to mobilise British public opinion for the overthrow of this pretty plot against world peace. The hordes of pacifists who overrun Britain during her present period of decadence were amazed and furious to wake up one morning and find staring at them from every vantage point the injunction: "Mind Britain's Business!" to be followed a few days later with a second, "Mosley Says Peace!" accompanied in every instance with the "flash of action in the circle of unity," the famous Blackshirt symbol. The Government mistook the shrieks of a few fake "intellectuals" for the voice of Britain, but at huge rallies throughout the land Mosley and his speakers were able to demonstrate the falsity of this view. His peace demonstrations, more than any other factor, kept the Government in check and blasted the war plans of the pacifist racketeers.

Now he moves forward to a still greater destiny, an implacable figure looming ever more immense against the background of his times; through his own eager spirit, so full of aspiration and boldness, symbolising the immortal spirit of his race.

If in the final decision gratitude is lacking for the advent of this "root and branch man," it will not be for the lack of a loyal following. In particular, those of the war-generations who believed that they fought for some other purpose than to make Britain a paradise for financial wolves and political jackals feel that they owe Mosley a debt of gratitude which not even the staunchest service can ever quite repay. It has long been clear to them that the contraption which passes for Britain's national life could not go on forever without afflicting the soul of the people with decay. In many a dark hour they have even wondered if it would not almost be preferable to witness the onrush of the Red destroyers instead of the slower processes of disintegration which are now well advanced upon their work. In the darkest of all hours, however, a great Englishman has come forward to relieve them of this disastrous choice, calling Britons to a revolution conforming all along the line to their own temperament - a revolution to destroy all that is putrid, but to preserve and enhance all that is fine; planning a future that shall combine whatever is great in the past with the inspiration of the modern creed: a revolution such as the world would expect from Britain, loyal to King and Country, but determined that both shall receive grander service in the days ahead. Mosley has transformed their bitterness into the nobler stuff of which their Blackshirt crusade is made. He has brought back the aspirations of manhood and given his followers once again the audacity to hope and to work, without which they can scarcely be said to have lived during the years of the post-war disillusionment and betrayal. Through his own example he has restored the heroic thing which is the spirit of Britain. If the hearts of his followers prove one-tenth as great as Mosley's heart, their courage one-tenth as high as his courage, they will not relinquish the struggle until the heights of Fascist power be won; until Britain's great revolutionary leader, sprung from one thousand years' contact with British soil, achieves power to act for and with the British people, in the name of their ancient sanity and splendour, that there may be built up in their peerless land a corporate life which shall ensure that her million hero-sons did not die to make a mock for history. Their battle-shout sounds above the discords and semi-tones of a fading age: Hail, Mosley, patriot, revolutionary, and leader of men!

www.ingramcontent.com/pod-product-compliance
Lightning Source LLC
Chambersburg PA
CBHW061733270326
41928CB00011B/2218